Setting Up a

Saltwater Aquarium

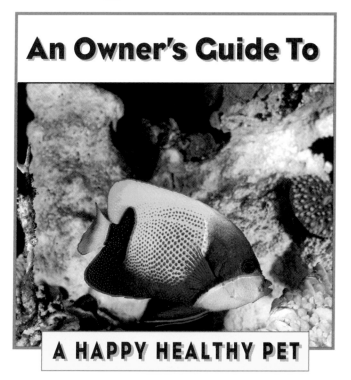

An Owner's Guide To

A HAPPY HEALTHY PET

Howell Book House

Howell Book House
A Simon & Schuster Macmillan Company
1633 Broadway
New York, NY 10019

Library of Congress Cataloging-in-Publication Data
Skomal, Gregory.
Setting up a saltwater aquarium : an owner's guide to a happy, healthy pet / Gregory Skomal.
p. cm
Includes bibliographical references.
ISBN 0-87605-529-3

1. Marine aquariums. 2. Tropical fish. I. Title.
SF457. 1.S585   1997
639.34'2—dc21   97-6612
                       CIP
Manufactured in the United Sates of America
10 9 8 7 6 5 4

Series Director: Ariel Cannon
Series Assistant Director: Jennifer Liberts
Book Design: Michele Laseau
Cover Design: Iris Jeromnimon
Illustration: Marvin Van Tiem
  Photography: Aaron Norman: 2-3, 6, 8, 11, 13, 16, 35, 43, 48, 49, 50-51, 52, 53, 54, 55, 59, 61, 63, 65, 66, 67, 68, 69, 70, 71, 72, 73, 74, 75, 76, 77, 78, 79, 80, 81, 82, 83, 84, 85, 88, 90-91, 92, 93, 94, 97, 99, 100, 101, 102, 104, 109, 113, 114, 119, 120, 121, 122
  Gregory Skomal: 7, 17, 23
  Bruce Webb: 20, 39
  Front and back cover photos by Aaron Norman
Production Team: Robyn Burnett, Kathleen Caulfield, Natalie Hollifield, Stephanie Hammett, and Stephanie Mohler

Contents

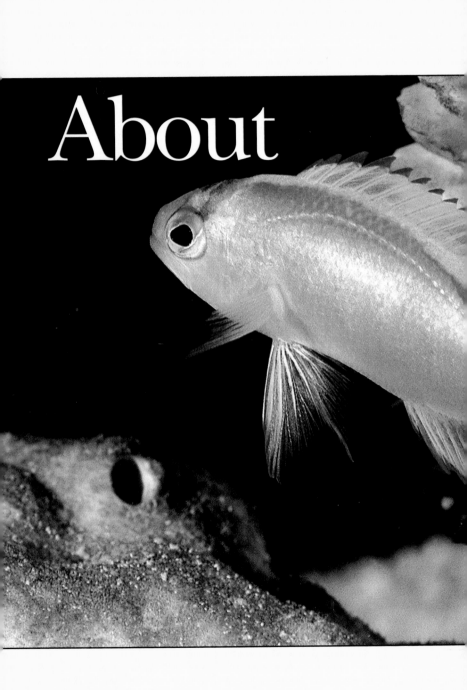

About

part one

Fish
and
Aquariums

External Features of the Saltwater Fish

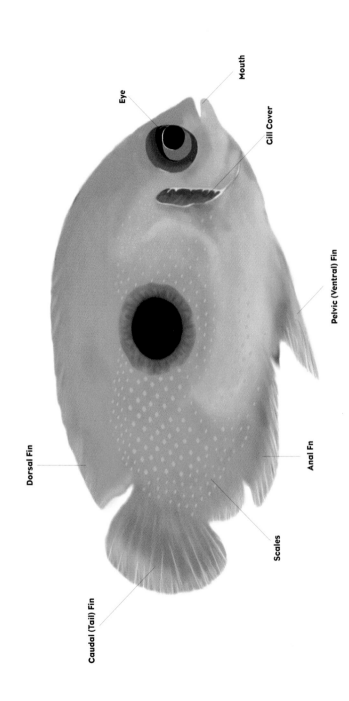

Eye

Mouth

Gill Cover

Pelvic (Ventral) Fin

Dorsal Fin

Anal Fin

Scales

Caudal (Tail) Fin

chapter 1

About
Marine Fish

You are reading this book because you are interested in owning and maintaining a saltwater aquarium. Perhaps you have had a freshwater tank and would like to graduate to the more complex marine environment. Like myself, you are a fish enthusiast. The world of fish is both fascinating and complex.

This book will help you to understand that world and will teach you what you need to know to set up and maintain a successful saltwater aquarium. Part of this requires a general knowledge of fish, their anatomy and biology. The rest centers on a thorough understanding of their proper care and husbandry. First, we will take a look at fish anatomy and what makes these animals so unique. Then we'll examine the aquarium and the importance of meeting the biological needs of fish. In doing so, the critical differences between freshwater

5

and saltwater aquariums will be fully described. We'll walk through the basics of aquarium setup and proper maintenance. We'll cover proper nutrition and feeding, fish health and disease and some advanced marine aquarium techniques. The only topic we will not discuss is saltwater fish breeding; so few have been successfully spawned in captivity that it is clearly an endeavor best left to the experts.

Aquarium Fish

The group of aquatic animals we call fish has evolved for over 400 million years to be the most numerous and diverse of the major vertebrate groups. Fish have permeated all the waters of the world, adapting an incredible variety of forms, lifestyles and behaviors. From the seasonal freshwater stream, desert spring and salty bay to the coral reef, open ocean and deep abyss, fish have found suitable niches. There are well over 20,000 species of fish that currently inhabit the earth and many more are being discovered every year.

Coral reef habitats have an abundance of fantastic fish, like this Fu Man Chu Lionfish.

Since salt water covers over 70 percent of the earth's surface and fresh water only 1 percent, you would expect that there would be many more marine (saltwater) species than freshwater species of fish. Surprisingly, only 58 percent of the world's fish species live exclusively in salt water. Of these, only 13 percent are associated with the open ocean. By far, the majority of marine species live in the narrow band of water less than 500 feet deep along the coastlines of land masses. As you move into warmer tropical waters, fish species diversify and the number of species dramatically increases. Fish that inhabit the warm waters of the coral reef are usually the most sought after for aquaria because of their incredible beauty. This book will address the characteristics, requirements and husbandry of these creatures.

Fish of the coral reef are sought after for their incredible beauty. Pictured here are grunts.

Saltwater vs. Freshwater Habitats

The fundamental differences between fresh- and salt-water fish lie in the two environmental extremes in which they live. In general, the freshwater species of fish are hardier than their marine counterparts, having evolved to withstand the rapid and dramatic changes in water conditions that occur inland. On the other hand, most marine species have lived in constant environmental conditions; they have not evolved the mechanisms to adapt to sudden changes, such as those that may occur in the home aquarium. This, of course, renders these fish more difficult to maintain in captivity.

Obviously, salt water contains much higher concentrations of salt (sodium chloride) than fresh water. In addition, many other dissolved elements occur in higher concentrations in salt water than they do in fresh water. The amount of these dissolved "salts" in water is referred to as its salinity. All living things must balance their internal chemistry within very precise limits in order to survive. In general, the salinity of cells must be maintained in the face of external salinity gradients. In the process called "osmosis," pure water flows through cell membranes from areas of low salinity to areas of high salinity. Fish in fresh water are constantly subjected to an influx of water because their cells are more saline than their environment. On the other hand, marine fish are always threatened by the loss of water from their cells because their environment is more saline.

Marine fish, like this Yellowback Fairy Basslet, expend a lot of energy keeping their bodies regulated in salt water.

Although marine and freshwater fish are anatomically similar in appearance, they have evolved very different ways of living in their respective environments. As a means of maintaining their internal salinity, freshwater fish drink very little water and produce large quantities of dilute urine. In contrast, most marine fish drink large quantities of water, and eliminate salts in small amounts of highly concentrated urine and feces, as well as at the gills. (Sharks and their close relatives, rays, are exceptions to this pattern in marine fish. These species concentrate urea in their tissues and blood to offset the loss of water.)

This aspect of water balance in the body of a fish relative to its external medium is called osmoregulation. It is important to understand the basic principles of osmoregulation because it has important implications for fish in captivity. Now you understand that freshwater fish cannot be kept in salt water because their bodies cannot adapt to the change. Since marine fish must expend a lot of energy to prevent the loss of water and excrete salt, they require good health and lots of food. Third, marine fish drink large amounts of water, and because the quality of water must be very good. Lastly, abrupt changes in salinity will disturb the internal chemistry of marine fish. For these reasons, marine fishkeeping can be more difficult than the maintenance of a freshwater system, but with a little extra effort, it can be infinitely rewarding.

Fish Anatomy

Despite the differences that allow marine fish to live in seawater, there are many similarities between freshwater and marine fish. Let's take a closer look at the unique adaptations of fish that have allowed them to live so successfully in the aquatic environment.

Because there are no less than 12,000 kinds of marine fish, it is difficult to describe the "typical" fish. For the most part, however, all fish have some common attributes. Since water is 800 times denser than air, fish have developed a variety of ways to move easily, breathe and feed in a dense medium. Anatomical adaptations include the body shape, fins, scales and swim bladder.

FISH ANATOMY

There are thousands of different species of fish, all uniquely adapted to their particular environments. However, most share fundamental characteristics that allow them to be classified together as fish.

Gills: These enable the fish to take in oxygen from the water.

Fins: These move the fish through the water, providing propulsion and steering.

Swim Bladder: This organ fills up with air, thereby controlling the fish's level in the water column.

Lateral Line: This sensory organ alerts the fish to movement close by. Helps fish in schools to move in synchronization.

Scales: These streamline and protect the body of the fish as it moves through the water.

Body Form

A great deal can be learned about a species of fish by looking at its body form or shape. Fish that are streamlined or bullet shaped are specially adapted to open waters, while flat or stocky fish are well adapted for living on or close to the bottom.

Fins

Almost all species of fish have fins in one form or another. The fins are critically important appendages that allow the fish to propel, stabilize, maneuver and stop. In some cases, fins have developed to protect the fish as well. A fish's fins can take on many shapes and functions depending on the type of fish and the habitat it lives in. Bottom, sedentary or slower moving fish possess rounded fins, while faster, open-water fish generally have longer, pointed fins.

Fins can be either paired or unpaired depending on the species of the fish and the function of the fin. The pectoral fins are the forwardmost paired fins. These fins help the fish stabilize, turn, maneuver, hover and swim backwards. The pectoral fins are generally found just behind or below the gills on each side of the fish under the midline of the body. The pelvic fins are also paired and are the most variable in position. In some fish, the pelvics lie under the fish toward the rear. In others, like many tropical fish, the pelvics are closer to the head under the pectorals. In general, the pelvic fins act as brakes while aiding in stabilizing and turning the fish. The dorsal and anal fins are unpaired fins, found protruding from the top and bottom of the fish behind the genital and anal openings, respectively. Dorsal fins may be elongated or short, elaborate or simple, singular or multiple. In some species of fish, the dorsal or anal fin may be completely lacking. Both fins help stabilize the fish and keep it moving straight. The caudal or tail fin is an unpaired fin that is largely responsible for propelling the fish forward. This fin is the source of forward momentum for most fish and can also assist in turning and braking. Tail shape will tell much about the lifestyle of a fish. Faster fish have deeply forked caudal fins while many deep-bodied and bottom fishes have square or rounded tails.

In general, the main supporting structures of fish fins are soft rays. However, anyone who has handled a fish knows that the dorsal, anal or pectoral fins of many species also have spines. These sharp bony structures provide protection against predators.

SCALES

The bodies of most fish are covered with scales. The scales are composed of a hard bony substance and serve to protect the fish, reducing the chance of injuries and infection. Covering the scales is a very thin layer of epidermal tissue that contains mucous cells. These cells produce the slimy texture we normally attribute to fish. The mucous coating on fish not only protects the fish against injury and infection but helps the fish swim more easily in the water, reducing the friction between the body and the surrounding water.

The bright colors of this Popeye Catalufa are created by chromatophores in the skin.

The scales of a fish are actually translucent and lack color. The source of the vibrant colors of tropical fish is specialized pigment cells called chromatophores in the dermal layer of the skin. Fish that are clear, like the freshwater Glassfish, lack these pigments. The color of the fish depends on the types of chromatophores present.

The bodies of sharks and rays are not covered with scales, but with tiny scalelike teeth called denticles. The denticles have a texture of sandpaper and serve the same functions as scales in other fish.

SWIM BLADDER

As mentioned earlier, living in the dense medium of water presents a few problems for fish: One of these is buoyancy. Maintaining a certain level in the water column without having to expend a lot of energy is very important to fish. To accomplish this, most species have special organs called swim bladders. This gas filled sac located in the abdominal cavity of the fish acts as a life vest, keeping the fish at the correct level in the water column. There are many types of swim bladders ranging from the simple single chambered sac of the trout to the three chambered bladder of the codfish. Some fish have a direct connection between the esophagus and the swim bladder and simply have to swallow air to fill it. Others must rely on gas exchange from specialized blood vessels in the circulatory system.

In addition to its role in buoyancy control, the swim bladder also helps to mechanically amplify sound for better hearing in certain species of fish.

Not all species of marine fish have swim bladders. For example, the sharks and their close relatives, the rays, have large fatty livers, instead of swim bladders, to help maintain buoyancy. Their skeletons are composed of cartilage which also reduces their density in water. Many species of tuna also lack swim bladders; their streamlined bodies and forward speed help them to maintain buoyancy.

FEEDING

Just as the body form of a fish can tell you a lot about its swimming habits, the mouth can tell you something about its feeding habits. Bottom feeders have downward pointing mouths while surface feeders have mouths that point up. For most fish, the mouth is at the end of the snout. The size of the mouth is usually directly related to the size of the fish's preferred food. For example, large predatory fish like sharks and barracuda have large mouths armed with teeth for consuming other fish. On the other hand, fish like Butterflyfish that normally feed on small aquatic invertebrates have smaller mouths.

Some tropical marine fish have specialized mouths for specialized feeding strategies. The sharp "beak" of the Parrotfish is helpful for feeding on the coral reef. The Basking Shark, which feeds on microscopic planktonic creatures, has a mouth that opens very wide and specialized gills that allow it to sift the water.

Fish that feed on small invertebrates, like this Copperband Butterflyfish, have small mouths appropriate to the size of their preferred food.

Most marine fish have a relatively straightforward digestive system which varies from species to species. In general, food passes from the mouth, down the esophagus, to the stomach, small and large intestines and out the anus. However, several species of fish lack true stomachs and have elongated, supercoiled intestines. Again, the sharks and rays are different in that they possess a specialized large intestine called the spiral valve.

BREATHING

Like land animals, fish are living creatures that require oxygen to live. However, instead of lungs, fish have specialized organs called gills that allow them to breathe. The gills of a fish are analogous to our lungs; they provide oxygen to and remove carbon dioxide from the

13

fish's blood. This oxygen is then transported by the blood to the tissues of the fish where it is utilized to produce energy. Water contains much less oxygen than air and fish must breathe ten to thirty times more water to get the same amount of oxygen that a land animal would get from air.

Most fish have four gills on each side of the head which are protected by a singular gill flap, or operculum. Sharks and their relatives possess five to seven gills, each with its own gill slit.

To breathe, water is taken into the mouth by the fish and passed over the gills and out the operculum. As water passes over the membranes and filaments of the gills, oxygen is removed and carbon dioxide is excreted. To accomplish this, the gills have a very high number of blood vessels which deliver the oxygen to the rest of the fish via the blood.

OTHER ORGANS

Aside from the notable exceptions outlined above, fish typically possess general circulatory, digestive, respiratory and nervous system features common to most vertebrates. Curious readers should examine the bibliography list in the back of the book for more detailed descriptions of the unique anatomy of fish.

Senses

With few exceptions, fish have no fewer than five senses which they use to feed, avoid predators, communicate and reproduce.

Sight

The eyes of most fishes are similar to our own, except that they lack eyelids and their irises work much more slowly. Some species of sharks, however, have specialized "eyelids" called nictitating membranes which protect the eyes. Rapid changes in light intensity tend to shock a fish and this should be taken into account by the aquarist. Gradual changes in light allow the fish to accommodate and avoid temporary blindness. The location of the spherical lenses of fish eyes renders most fish nearsighted. Although it varies from species to species, fish can detect color.

Sound

Water is a much more efficient conductor of sound than air is. Therefore, sound carries much farther and faster in water than in air. Most fish do not possess external ears, but instead have an inner ear structure not noticeable on the outside.

Smell

Fish have external nasal passages called nares that allow water to pass into and out of the olfactory organ located above its mouth and below its eyes. Water flows through the nares and into the olfactory pits where odors are perceived and communicated to the brain via a large nerve. The olfactory system of the fish is not attached to the respiratory system like it is in humans, but remains isolated from the mouth and gills. Smell is particularly important in prey and mate detection in fish.

Taste

This is generally a close range sense in fish and is especially helpful in the identification of both food and noxious substances. In addition to being in the mouth, the taste buds of fishes are located on several external surfaces like their skin, lips and fins. Catfish have specialized barbels studded with taste buds that help them detect food in murky waters.

Touch

Fish have very specialized organs comprising the lateral line system which allows them to detect water movements. Sensory receptors lying along the surface of the fish's body in pits or grooves detect water displacement and give the fish a sensation of touch. The lateral line is easily visible along the sides of most fish. This unique system helps the fish detect other fish and avoid obstacles.

chapter 2

About
Aquariums

Queen Angelfish

It is no surprise that man has favored keeping fish in captivity for centuries. The common goldfish was kept in captivity in China as long ago as 265 A.D. Care and husbandry of fish has come a long way over the centuries and in recent years there has been an incredible explosion of fish culture for aquarium hobbyists.

There was a time when most tropical fish kept in captivity were taken from their native homes. This practice contributed to the degradation of tropical habitats and the local depletion of many species. Fortunately, modern husbandry techniques have taken tremendous pressure off natural stocks and many of the common freshwater aquarium species are bred in captivity. Selective breeding has also allowed for the rearing of hardier fish that are more adaptive to the varying water conditions of the aquarium.

16

Although they represent only a fraction of the number of ornamental fishes sold, almost all of the saltwater species are harvested from the wild. The most popular of these fish come primarily from coral reef ecosystems. If managed properly, the coral reefs around the world can be harvested without harm. Coral reef systems are extremely productive because of their size and the competitive nature of the inhabitants. Care should be taken, however, not to purchase fish that may have been harvested in areas that do not adhere to sound conservation of natural reefs.

Fish can be safely harvested from coral reefs if this is done in adherence to strict conservation techniques.

Fish in their natural environment are subjected to many challenges in order to survive. Most of these involve natural processes of predation, feeding, reproduction and disease. Natural catastrophic events that alter water quality are rare, and fish can generally avoid them by moving to other areas. In many ways, fish in the wild are very much responsible for themselves. (A possible exception to this would be fish living in areas assaulted by manmade pollution.)

Fish maintained in an artificial environment like an aquarium are also faced with challenges in order to survive. However, most of these challenges cannot be met by the fish and must be met by the fishkeeper. When you take it upon yourself to set up an aquarium, you are accepting the responsibility of meeting all of the needs of all the inhabitants. This involves maintaining high water quality, proper feeding, correct water temperature, a balanced fish community of the proper density, appropriate habitat and shelter and sufficient lighting, to name a few. The fish are totally dependent upon you. If they get sick or diseased, you must treat them. As you gain experience as a fishkeeper, you may go beyond the basic needs and start to breed your fish or establish specialty tanks, but first, it's important to start slowly with your aquarium and develop your talents as an aquarist. You will learn a tremendous amount through your own experiences. If you are an experienced freshwater aquarist, you will learn that marine fish are less tolerant of suboptimal water quality conditions and you must be meticulous in the quality of your care. Be sure to keep records of all your experiences.

Meeting the Needs of Your Fish

Before you purchase your aquarium supplies and fish, try to visit all the local aquarium stores before you choose one or two to work with. If you have worked successfully with a freshwater aquarium dealer, this would be the logical place to start with your marine interests. It is very important to establish a good working relationship with your aquatic dealer because you will need someone to advise you during the setup and maintenance of your system. You want somebody who maintains a good clean business, has healthy fish in the store, and is always willing to answer your questions and spend time with you. The good dealer will give you invaluable information about new and reliable products. He or she will *want* to help you maintain your system correctly. Try to avoid dealers who will not take the time to explain things to you or net the specific fish you desire. I've always preferred the pet shops that cater to the needs of all levels, are willing to special order supplies and would rather send you elsewhere than sell you an improper choice. When you settle on one or two dealers, you are then ready to begin planning your aquarium.

THE FISH TANK

Before you choose your aquarium setup, take the time to plan every aspect of its use. Determine beforehand where you are going to put the aquarium. To avoid excessive algal growth, avoid placing the aquarium in direct sunlight. Make sure that the structure of the building will hold the full aquarium. Water weighs about 8.4 pounds per gallon so a 30 gallon tank will weigh 250 pounds, not including gravel and other furnishings. Choose a location that has an adequate electrical supply and is not too far from a source of water. Well used living areas provide excellent settings for aquariums because the fish acclimate to people entering and leaving the room. Keeping the aquarium in a rarely used area will render fish skittish and timid when people approach the tank. Lastly, choose a location that can tolerate a water spill. Even the most meticulous of aquarists will spill water around an aquarium and in many cases water will be splashed from a tank. Think carefully about where the tank will be placed because once the aquarium is set up, it cannot be easily moved.

> **TANK TIPS**
>
> The following are some basic things to keep in mind when choosing your aquarium tank.
>
> - choose the largest tank you can afford and accommodate
> - choose a long rectangular tank rather than a tall one
> - never use a goldfish bowl
> - choose glass rather than acrylic
> - make sure there are no gaps in the sealant

Tank Size

The general rule of thumb is to buy the largest tank that you can afford and accommodate in your home. The reason for this is fairly straightforward. Fish require adequate space to swim and sufficient oxygen to live; both are determined by the size of the tank. The oxygen content of water is related to the surface area of the tank and the temperature of the water. Warmer water has less oxygen than colder water. Since most marine tropical fish prefer water in excess of 75 degrees F, the amount of oxygen may be limited in the tank. The more surface area a tank has, the more room for gas exchange at the surface. This means more oxygen entering the water and more toxic gases leaving the water. Therefore, the larger the tank the more fish the tank can hold.

You'll want to consider at this point how many fish to keep in the tank. Most aquarists use fish length and tank volume to estimate the number of fish that a marine aquarium can hold. Larger fish consume more oxygen and, therefore, require more aquarium space. The general rule of thumb is 1 inch (2.5 cm) of fish per 4 gallons (18 liters) of water for the first six months. Gradually increase fish density to 1 inch per 2 gallons (9 liters) after this initial period. For example, a 40 gallon aquarium should contain no more than 10 inches of fish for the first six months. These may be comprised of one 3 inch Queen Angel, two 1 inch Clownfish, one 2 inch Regal Tang, one 1 inch Bicolor Blenny and three 1 inch Beau Gregories. After six months, additional fish may be added gradually to increase the total number of inches to 20.

Buy the largest size aquarium you can afford and, ideally, purchase it with a sturdy stand.

Because surface area is so important to the capacity and health of your aquarium, long tanks are much better than tall tanks. Even though both tanks may hold the same volume of water, the upright (tall) tank will have a much lower carrying capacity of fish because of its smaller surface area. The minimal starter tank for the saltwater aquarium should be 30 gallons.

Once you have decided on the appropriate size of your aquarium, choosing the tank itself is very straightforward. Most home aquariums are constructed of rectangular glass plates sealed with a silicone rubber cement. These are by far the most common and practical aquarium to buy; I recommend one for the beginner. They are built for the sole purpose of housing living animals and are, therefore, nontoxic. Glass does not scratch or yellow as easily as acrylic does. Aquariums with plastic or metal frames are sometimes available, but I have found that this design is not as aesthetically pleasing and that the frames are unnecessary. Seawater is extremely corrosive, so tanks with metal frames will corrode, rendering the tank unsafe and potentially adding toxic metals to the aquarium water.

When choosing you tank, be sure there are no scratches on the glass and that there are no gaps in the silicone. Enthusiasts who have tanks custom built or who build their own must be sure that non-toxic silicone cement is used to seal the glass.

The Aquarium Stand

The best support for the heavy weight of the aquarium and all its components is a commercially manufactured aquarium stand. This type of support is built to hold a full aquarium. Homemade stands and common household furniture may look sturdy, but can fail under the heavy load. Stand failure can be costly to both the aquarist and the homeowner so don't try to save money on your support for the aquarium.

If you decide not to buy a commercially built stand, place a $^5/_8''$ sheet of plywood and a $^1/_2''$ sheet of polystyrene cut to the dimensions of the tank under the tank. These layers will even out any imperfections in the supporting surface and distribute the load of the tank.

The Tank Hood

An essential item for any aquarium is a hood (canopy or cover). This important piece of equipment performs a variety of functions. First, it prevents unwanted items from entering the tank and injuring the fish. Second, it prevents overzealous fish from jumping out of the tank. (Remember, fish cannot breathe air and nothing is worse than finding your pet on the floor next to the aquarium in the morning.) Third, the cover prevents water from splashing to the walls and floor causing damage. Fourth, the hood slows the rate of water evaporation from the tank. Water will condense on the cover and re-enter the tank instead of evaporating into the room. This limits the necessity of adding more water. When water evaporates from a seawater aquarium, the salts do not leave the tank, but become more concentrated, thereby increasing the salinity. This will disturb the fish and the water quality if not carefully monitored. Fifth, the hood helps the aquarium retain heat thereby reducing the use of the heating unit. Lastly, the hood keeps water from damaging the aquarium light and prevents a potentially dangerous electrical problem.

The hood is generally fitted to the dimensions of the tank and can be adjusted to allow for aquarium accessories. Make sure it is composed of thick $^1/8''$ glass or plastic so it can support the weight of other aquarium components if needed. Also, it should be segmented so the entire assembly need not be removed to feed the fish or work in the tank. For the beginner, I strongly recommend the type of hood that also houses the aquarium light. These units are self contained and properly designed to keep water from the lighting unit, minimize danger and thoroughly cover the entire tank. I've always felt that the tank, stand and hood should be built by the same manufacturer and purchased as a package. This insures against the mismatching of aquarium components and may be less expensive to the beginner.

THE FILTER

The most important requirement of healthy fish is clean water. Fish in the natural marine environment are generally exposed to an open system where water quality is not a problem. Products of respiration and digestion are readily swept away and naturally filtered. The sheer volume of water keeps these substances at levels that are virtually nonexistent.

In contrast, fish housed in the aquarium live in a closed system where products of respiration and digestion remain until they are removed. The primary piece of equipment that removes toxic substances from the aquarium is the filter. Before we discuss filtration and the types of filters available to the aquarist, it is important to examine the attributes of water quality and the natural wastes of fish.

In the open ocean clean water is not a problem, but in the closed system of the aquarium the filter bears responsibility for keeping the water clean.

As mentioned earlier, marine fish are accustomed to much more stable environmental conditions than their freshwater counterparts. They are more sensitive to even small amounts of toxins and, hence, are more difficult to keep in captivity. Therefore, the most important thing is water quality. For the purposes of the aquarium keeper, water quality requires monitoring and occasionally adjusting several water parameters: water composition, pH, salinity and nitrogenous substance levels.

Seawater Composition

The chemical composition of seawater is consistent throughout the world. Although seawater is 96 percent pure water (H_2O), it also contains many dissolved minerals. Eighty-five percent of the mineral content is sodium and chlorine but magnesium, sulphate, calcium and potassium comprise another 13 percent, and bicarbonate and sixty-eight other elements make up the remainder in trace quantities.

The beginner is naturally inclined to try to obtain natural seawater for the home aquarium. However, for several reasons, I would strongly recommend that you use one of the synthetic salt mixes that are available at your pet store. First, if you do not live in the tropics and intend to maintain a tropical aquarium, your local seawater will be colder. The colder water will contain species of plankton that are adapted to these temperatures. Elevating the temperature to tropical levels will cause these organisms to die or rapidly proliferate, yielding polluted or poor quality water. Second, the logistics of travel back and forth to the seashore for large quantities of water will ultimately render its use impractical. Last, there are no guarantees that your water source is free of pollution. Seemingly clean seawater may contain high levels of toxic compounds and metals. Why take chances?

The science of marine chemistry has yielded salt mixes that mimic the marine environment without the potential toxins. These mixes can be dissolved in ordinary tap water and are perfectly suitable for the home aquarium. You should always mix up additional properly balanced salt water for water changes and emergencies. Batches of salt water should be stored in non-metallic containers in cool, dark places until needed.

Salinity

Marine species are adapted to a very specific level of dissolved salts in the water they inhabit. Therefore, the amount of dissolved salts, or salinity, in the water must be maintained at this level. However, to directly measure salinity, you need equipment that can be expensive for the average aquarist. The easiest and more practical way to measure the salinity in your tank is to measure "specific gravity." Technically, specific gravity refers to the ratio of densities of seawater to pure water at various temperatures. Pure water has a specific gravity of 1.000. For example, a specific gravity of 1.021 is 1.021 times denser than pure water.

We use a hydrometer to measure specific gravity in the aquarium. This is an essential piece of equipment for the marine aquarist to use every couple of days. The hydrometer can be of the floating tube type or needle type; the latter is easier to read.

Specific gravity should be established in the range of 1.021 and 1.024, but more importantly, it should be maintained at a very specific level within this range. Even minor fluctuations can cause problems for your tank inhabitants.

The greatest cause of salinity change is evaporation from the tank. When water evaporates in a marine aquarium, the salts remain in solution and the water becomes more concentrated, thereby increasing the salinity and specific gravity. You must constantly monitor water levels in the aquarium to prevent these fluctuations. Evaporation is easily remedied by adding *fresh water* to the tank, not additional salt water. Don't wait until levels have significantly dropped before you top off the tank. Instead do so regularly with small quantities from the tap.

There can be some loss of salt from the tank due to crystallization on the hood and other fixtures and losses from the protein skimmer. Keep an eye on the hydrometer. Nonetheless, water evaporation occurs faster than salt loss.

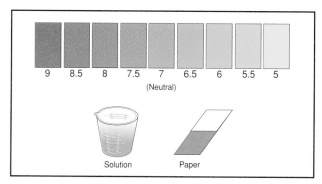

pH levels.

pH

The pH refers to the amount of acidity of the water. It ranges from 0 to 14 with a pH of 7 being neutral, a pH of 1 being very acidic and a pH of 14 being very alkaline. This scale is logarithmic, meaning that each number is ten times stronger than the preceding number. For example, a pH of 2 is ten times more acidic than a pH of 3 and 100 times more acidic than a pH of 4.

Salt water is more alkaline than fresh water. If you had a freshwater aquarium, you probably maintained the pH within the range of 6.5 to 7.5. On the other hand, the pH of seawater is about 8.2, and should be maintained in the aquarium between 8.1 and 8.3.

pH is influenced by a variety of factors including the amount of carbon dioxide and fish wastes in the water. The accumulation of either or both of these will cause the water to acidify and the pH to drop. Commercial test kits that are very simple to use are available at most pet stores. This water parameter should be monitored every week or two to detect any changes. An abrupt drop in pH may be indicative of an increase of carbon dioxide or nitrogenous fish wastes. An increase in aeration and a partial water change will be necessary to alleviate the problem before the lives of tank inhabitants are compromised.

The Nitrogen Cycle

Fish are living creatures that obtain energy from food and burn that energy with the help of oxygen which they obtain from the water. These processes generate waste products which are returned to the environment via the gills and the anus. These wastes are primarily carbon dioxide and nitrogenous compounds like ammonia, which are extremely toxic to fish. In the aquarium, these wastes must be removed. Carbon dioxide generally leaves the water through aeration at the surface or through photosynthesis by aquarium algae. Toxic nitrogenous compounds like ammonia and nitrite are converted to less toxic compounds via the nitrogen cycle.

The nitrogen cycle involves the conversion of toxic nitrogenous wastes and ammonia into harmless products by bacterial colonies. In short, species of bacteria convert solid wastes excreted by fish into ammonia,

ammonia into nitrite and nitrite into nitrate. In nature, nitrate may be utilized by algae as fertilizer or converted to nitrogen gas by bacteria and removed from the water. In most aquarium systems, nitrate will slowly accumulate in the water because there is not enough algae and bacteria present to utilize nitrate or convert it to nitrogen gas. These nitrates must eventually be removed and this is done during frequent 10 percent water changes.

A healthy aquarium depends greatly on the nitrogen cycle to convert toxic ammonia into less toxic nitrogen compounds. This cycle can only be properly established in a **biological filter,** which is a requirement for all marine aquariums (see below). Even with a properly functioning biological filter, the levels of ammonia, nitrite and nitrate should be monitored frequently by the aquarist. This can be done with commercial test kits

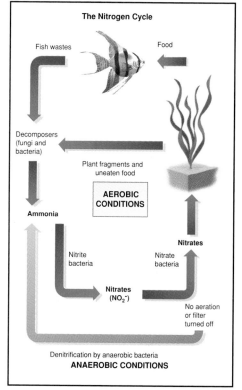

The Nitrogen Cycle

Fish wastes

Food

Decomposers (fungi and bacteria)

Plant fragments and uneaten food

AEROBIC CONDITIONS

Ammonia

Nitrite bacteria

Nitrate bacteria

Nitrates

Nitrates (NO$_2^-$)

No aeration or filter turned off

Denitrification by anaerobic bacteria
ANAEROBIC CONDITIONS

that are available at your pet store. Make sure to purchase a test kit that can be used for both fresh and salt water because you want to be able to test the quality of your tap water before using it for your aquarium.

Types of Filters

In natural systems, nitrogen compounds are readily removed from the fish's habitat. In the aquarium, this is accomplished by the filtration system. There are three basic types of filtration: mechanical, chemical and biological.

Mechanical filters physically remove suspended particles from the water by passing it through a fine filter medium, which sifts out the particles. External power filters and canister filters provide rapid mechanical filtration. **Chemical filtration** involves the chemical treatment of water to remove toxic substances. When you add activated carbon to an external power filter, you are providing chemical filtration. **Biological filtration** utilizes the nitrogen cycle to remove toxic compounds from the water. An excellent example of a biological filter is the undergravel filter that draws water through the aquarium substrate. This substrate contains the necessary bacteria to convert nitrogenous wastes to nitrate. Although this type of filtration requires some time to establish a viable working bacteria colony, it provides the best kind of filtration.

Most commercially manufactured aquarium filters provide all three kinds of filtration. For example, the external power filter will mechanically remove particles, chemically remove toxins if it contains activated carbon and biologically convert nitrogenous wastes via the nitrogen cycle in its filter media.

Some of the basic kinds of filters available to the beginner include the internal box filter, the external power filter, the external canister filter and the undergravel filter. For the marine aquarist, advanced filtration systems are rapidly being developed. These include trickle filters, protein skimmers and external water management filters. In addition, water sterilization techniques are also available in the form of ultraviolet (UV) sterilizers and ozonators. Choosing the right system for your new aquarium can be a bit confusing given all the different kinds and

THE FISHKEEPER'S RESPONSIBILITIES

The fishkeeper (that's you) has an obligation to care for the fish he or she has brought home. Because the fish are contained in an artificial environment, it is up to you to establish and maintain their living space in an appropriate manner. The fishkeeper is responsible for providing:

- high water quality

- proper feeding

- correct water temperature

- a balanced fish community of the proper density

- appropriate habitat and shelter

- sufficient lighting

Make sure you are ready to accept these responsibilities and the daily chores that go with them before you start setting up your aquarium.

manufacturers. Here is a brief description of each type with the pros and cons. For the marine aquarium, I thoroughly recommend multiple filter systems which include all three types of filtration.

Inside Box Filter   As the name implies, the inside box filter sits inside the aquarium. An external air pump drives air through the box drawing water from the aquarium and through fibrous filter media and activated charcoal. Layers of filter media provide mechanical and chemical filtration as well as adequate substrate for biological filtration. Because it is driven by air, this filter circulates and aerates the water. While the box filter may be suitable for the 10 gallon freshwater tank, it does not provide adequate levels of filtration for the marine aquarium. It is simply too small and inefficient to handle the wastes and debris that accumulate in the tank.

External Power Filter   The external power filter is the easiest and least complicated filter system for the beginner aquarist to employ. These filters provide all three kinds of filtration and are specifically designed to turn over large amounts of water. The external power filter hangs on the side of the tank and is powered by its own motor. Water is drawn into the filter by a U-shaped siphon tube where it passes over layers of fibrous filter material and activated carbon. Water is returned to the tank via a gravity trickle system or a return pipe. While it works on the same premises as the box filter, the power filter is much more efficient at removing wastes and debris from the tank. It does not need to be cleaned as frequently as the box filter. Newer models have specialized filter cartridges which make cleaning these filters extremely easy. In addition, there are various types of cartridges available that chemically alter water quality and correct water chemistry problems. Like the box filter, the power filter circulates the water providing aeration.

External canister filter   This is the next step up in power filters. This filter is much larger than the others and is designed to filter much larger tanks of

50 gallons or more. The canister filter is composed of a large jarlike canister that generally sits next to the tank. It contains filter media and activated carbon like the other filters but has a much more powerful motor for filtering large amounts of water. Water is drawn by an intake suction line and sent back to the aquarium through a return line. Water circulation can be provided by these filters if the return line is properly positioned. I only recommend this kind of filter for the aquarist with the larger tank.

Undergravel Filter   The undergravel filter is considered by many to be the most effective basic filter because it provides biological filtration. In my opinion, it is a must for every marine aquarium. This filter consists of a plastic plate that sits under the gravel (substrate) of the tank. Water is drawn through the gravel by pumping air to the bottom of the filter with an external air pump. Newer undergravel filters are driven by powerheads mounted on the intake tubes. Both kinds provide excellent water circulation, but make sure that the latter have air diffusers to provide aeration. In essence, this filter uses the aquarium gravel itself as the filter media. Thus, very little mechanical filtration is involved and chemical filtration is completely absent. The undergravel filter relies chiefly on the establishment of a healthy bacterial colony in the gravel. For this reason, certain kinds of gravel are required for this filter and a longer setup time is necessary to establish bacterial colonies. However, once a healthy filtration system is established, this filter can be used for months without intense maintenance and cleaning. Although this system provides the most valuable kind of filtration, it may seem the most complicated to the beginner. Nonetheless, the undergravel filter in combination with an external power filter is the standard of most marine aquariums.

Some aquarists prefer to modify the undergravel filter by reversing the flow of water through it with an external canister filter. In this system, water is pulled from the aquarium through the canister filter where it is mechanically and chemically filtered and then driven down the "uplift" tube, into the undergravel filter plate and out the aquarium substrate. These reverse flow undergravel filters prevent the substrate from clogging with debris. However, they do not provide adequate water circulation and supplemental water pumps or aerators are generally required.

Trickle filters   Beyond the basic system, trickle filters are generally recommended for the advanced aquarist that may have larger more sophisticated aquarium systems. The trickle filter provides the greatest biological filtration by drawing water from the tank, and exposing it to air and wide surface areas of aerobic bacteria before returning it to the aquarium. This system in combination with mechanical filtration is extremely effective. Although trickle filters are commercially available, most are built by advanced aquarists.

Protein Skimmers   Once only for the advanced marine aquarium, the protein skimmer is now commercially available for all saltwater enthusiasts. This piece of equipment utilizes "foam fractionation" to remove dissolved organic wastes from the water. Basically, the protein skimmer is a tube that hangs in the back of your tank. Air is pushed to the bottom of the tube, generating a cloud of very fine bubbles which flow to the surface. Protein and other wastes adhere to the bubbles, travel to the surface, and collect in a removable cup that is emptied. Most inexpensive models are driven by an air pump, which also moves water through the unit, aerating it. The protein skimmer can remove considerable amounts of waste and is thoroughly recommended for the beginner as well the advanced aquarist. Make sure that your protein skimmer extends the height of the tank to maximize efficiency and works countercurrent to water flow.

Water Management Systems   It is possible now to buy complete water management systems for your new aquarium that incorporate the biological filtration of trickle filters with chemical and mechanical filters, heaters, aerators, nitrate removers and protein skimmers. These units can be very expensive, but represent the future of water quality management in the home aquarium. Before you purchase your aquarium components, it may be worth looking into one of these new systems.

Water Disinfection   There are two common methods for disinfecting water that are commercially available to the home aquarist, UV sterilizers and ozonators. Although some authors recommend one or both of them for the marine aquarium, I do not think that they are necessary for the beginner.

UV sterilizers are self-contained units that kill some microorganisms that may be harmful to your fishes. Water is passed from your power filter to the UV unit, where it is exposed to ultraviolet light before being returned to the tank. However, the effectiveness of this method depends on many factors and its utility for the home aquarist has been questioned. UV disinfection is recommended only if you intend to maintain delicate species of fish and only to treat severe outbreaks of disease.

Ozonators produce ozone which kills microorganisms in the aquarium. However, the chemistry of ozone in seawater is poorly understood and ozone can be harmful to humans. Therefore, the beginner is urged not to use ozonators for water disinfection.

Live Rock   The use of live rock as a filtration method is becoming increasingly popular in the aquarium trade. Live rock is a piece of dead coral encrusted with many forms of living plants and animals. These living things provide high levels of natural biological filtration. Some aquarists rely solely on live rock and an external power filter, bypassing the use of an undergravel filter. I recommend this route only if you have an experienced, qualified dealer to assist you.

AERATION

Although most filters provide water circulation and aeration to the aquarium, it is a very good idea to have an external air pump moving air through one or more airstones in the tank. Fish need to have a lot of oxygen available for respiration. This is especially true for tanks at their fullest carrying capacity of fish. The air pump will increase circulation in the tank, promote oxygen exchange at the surface and increase the escape of carbon dioxide, carbon monoxide and free ammonia from the tank. In addition, this increase in circulation will act to mix all the aquarium levels so that a uniform temperature is maintained throughout the tank.

There are two general air pumps designs: the diaphragm type and the piston type. The former is much more common and will generally provide enough maintenance-free usage for the beginner's aquarium. The piston pump, however, is more powerful and should be used in larger aquariums and if an undergravel filter and multiple airstones need to be powered. The size and power output of air pumps vary. Consult your local dealer to match your aquarium with the proper air pump.

The airstone is generally made of porous rock which allows air to pass through it splitting the airstream into tiny bubbles. Too fine a mist will cause bubbles to adhere to various tank decorations and to fish. You want the bubbles to slowly travel to the surface and agitate the water.

Your air pump and airstones will require an air hose to form the link between the two. This is plastic tubing that will deliver air from your pump to the airstone. This should fit snugly at all joints so that air does not escape from the system. Air leaks will reduce the efficiency of the system and may ultimately burn out the pump. Make sure that the tubing is manufactured for use in the aquarium; other types may be toxic to fish.

If you intend to run multiple airstones or additional devices like filters from a single pump, you will need one or more air valves. These will enable air flow to be directed to multiple devices from a single pump. The use of several air valves will allow you to turn on and shut off devices as you see fit.

THE HEATER

As I mentioned earlier, one of the basic attributes of water that fish have adapted to over time is temperature. Fish are sometimes grouped in general categories based on their temperature preferences. Temperate fish include many species that inhabit cooler waters. However, those fish most commonly seen in the marine aquarium are the tropical coral reef species. The term tropical refers to natural habitats where the waters are warm throughout the year. It should come as no surprise, therefore, that it is necessary to maintain your aquarium within a specific temperature range. This is the job of the aquarium heater. This essential piece of equipment will maintain your tank at a constant temperature regardless of the room temperature. Unless you are planning to set up a coldwater aquarium of temperate fishes, the species you be will keeping as a beginner will require that the aquarium temperature be maintained at 75 to 79 degrees F (24 to 26 degrees C). However, this is entirely species dependent and you should consult your local pet dealer or one of the many fish encyclopedias (see chapter 11) for specific temperature requirements. Make sure that you do not mix species that have very different temperature preferences. Also, temperature, like pH, must be maintained with little fluctuation so as not to stress your tank inhabitants.

There are several kinds of aquarium heaters available to the aquarist but the most common is the submersible glass tubular heater with a built-in thermostat. This heater attaches to the side of the tank and has external controls. Once it is properly set, it will automatically respond to changes in water temperature and turn on and off. Newer models have temperature dials that are preset by the manufacturer. Temperature is easily selected by the user. If one of these is to be used, I recommend that the aquarist double-check the accuracy of the dial with a thermometer.

In general, you should place your heater close to an area of high circulation so that heated water can be rapidly and evenly distributed throughout the tank. This is usually near the filter system or the airstones. The fully submersible heater can be placed at the bottom of the tank so heating convection can be optimized.

Heater size is largely dependent on the size of the aquarium. The general rule is 5 watts of power for every gallon of water in an unheated room. However, most home aquariums are kept in heated rooms where temperatures do not drop suddenly and dramatically. Thus, high wattage heaters are not required. A good rule of thumb is about 3 watts per gallon for heated rooms. Thus, a 30 gallon tank would require a 100 watt heater. Many experts recommend that two heaters be used in larger aquariums over 50 gallons. This will allow for the more even distribution of heat in the aquarium and will also maintain correct temperatures if one heater fails. The calculated wattage should be divided between the heaters (75 gallons would require two 100 watt heaters).

The marine fish in your aquarium will most likely be tropical, like this Peppermint Wrasse, and will need the temperature maintained between 75 degrees and 79 degrees F.

As with all electrical components, please handle your heater with extreme care. Do not switch you submersible heater on until it is submersed in water. Keep all of your electrical components unplugged until the tank is completely set up and full.

In order to maintain your water temperature at suitable levels, all aquarists need an accurate thermometer. There are basically two kinds of thermometers for the aquarium: the internal floating or fixed kind and the external stick-on kind. The former type tends to be more accurate since the latter has a tendency to read a

35

couple of degrees too low. This piece of equipment ex-
emplifies the kind of thing that is of the utmost importance to the aquarium yet does not cost a lot. Therefore,
two thermometers will allow you to carefully monitor
your aquarium temperature as well as to compare the
accuracy of each unit. Don't cut corners when it comes
to maintaining water quality and water temperature.

THE LIGHT

Proper lighting is a necessary component of every
aquarium because it provides illumination and it promotes algal growth. While lighting from the sun
provides a natural setting, it will also promote excessive
algal growth and alter temperature, so aquariums
should be placed away from sunlit areas. Instead, the
beginner aquarist should purchase a commercially
manufactured aquarium light to illuminate the tank.

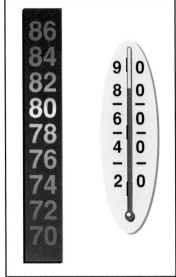

Like all aquarium components, these
come in a variety of types and forms.

By far, the most common is the fluorescent light that fits snugly on top
of the aquarium hood and evenly
provides cool illumination. There
are several types of fluorescent bulbs
that may be purchased to create special effects in your aquarium. Full
spectrum white tubes mimic natural
daylight and are the most suitable
for the fish-only marine aquarium.
Unlike in a freshwater tank, the
marine aquarist should promote the
growth of some green algae in the
aquarium. These algae not only consume carbon dioxide and nitro-

*Two kinds of
thermometers.*

genous wastes, but also produce oxygen and provide
food to some aquarium inhabitants. Marine tanks
intended to harbor invertebrates should have lighting
that promotes lush algal growth. The new triphospher
and actinic tubes are ideal for these aquaria. Your pet
shop dealer will carry a full variety of fluorescent light
bulbs.

If you purchase your fish tank with a hood and light canopy as I recommended, the latter will most often be a fluorescent light. If you do not purchase a tank, cover and light package, make sure the light you buy separately extends the entire length of the tank. This is by far the most efficient and economical form of lighting available for your tank and I thoroughly recommend it for the beginner aquarist.

Other types of lighting include incandescent, sodium, mercury vapor, metal halide and tungsten lights. These provide unique lighting opportunities, but tend to heat the water and are not as economical as fluorescent lights.

An often overlooked component of the lighting system is an on/off time switch. Tropical marine fish come from regions where daylight lengths range from 10 to 15 hours. A time switch will automatically turn on and shut off your lighting system so that a consistent day length can be maintained. A 12-hour day length is generally recommended for most aquariums. With regard to lighting, efforts should be made to keep from startling fish with sudden switching of the light on and off. To better simulate a normal sunset, you should switch off the aquarium light about an hour before other room lights are turned off. This little detail will help keep your fish happy and, therefore, healthy.

Inside the Tank

As I have emphasized throughout this book, the majority of marine aquarium inhabitants originate from tropical coral reef habitats. This being the case, I will limit my discussion of tank decoration to the mimicry of this type of ecosystem. Advanced aquarists often make great efforts to duplicate specific reef systems like those of Hawaii or the Caribbean, but this requires both experience and time. Since your basic marine community aquarium will feature a variety of fishes from multiple habitats, it is best to create an aquascape that is pleasing to the human eye as well as pleasing to the fish. This will require a variety of components that will go into your aquarium and meet the habitat needs of its inhabitants.

GRAVEL

The bottom substrate of your aquarium will consist of gravel. However, unlike the gravel in a freshwater aquarium, gravel in the saltwater tank must be of a specific type. Types of calcareous gravel have proven to be the most suitable substrate for the marine aquarium. These include coral gravel, dolomite, calcite and crushed oyster shell. These all contain carbonate which is thought to help "buffer" the seawater and, therefore, maintain pH levels.

Grain size and gravel depth are very important assuming that you will be using an undergravel filter. The depth of the gravel should be 3 inches with an average grain size of about 2 to 5 millimeters (.08 to .2 inches). This substrate will be the biological filter that drives the nitrogen cycle in your aquarium. Some authors recommend the use of two sizes of gravel (fine on top of coarse) separated by a plastic mesh or "gravel tidy." This may allow for filtration while minimizing the amount of substrate that can become clogged. The gravel tidy also protects the filter from burrowing tank inhabitants.

It is always best to buy a bit of extra gravel so that when you aquascape your tank, you have sufficient amounts to sculpt the bottom and provide relief.

ALGAE

Plants become an integral part of the freshwater aquarium, but are somewhat rare in the saltwater tank. This is because with few exceptions, all of the ocean's plant life are classified in the primitive group known as algae. The term seaweed actually refers to the many-celled forms of algae, and these are not common in the beginner's home aquarium. Plastic seaweeds are available and some marine hobbyists like their plant-like appearance. Experienced aquarists find the various species of *Caulerpa* algae to be attractive additions to the tank.

CORAL

By far the best decoration for the tropical marine aquarium is coral and artificial coral replicas. These structures give the aquarium a natural look, provide excellent shelter for tank inhabitants and are an ideal substrate for algal growth. Real coral and other calcareous objects like shells also provide the added benefit of buffering the water for pH maintenance.

Coral is basically the skeletal remains of millions of living animals that lived as a colony. In a natural coral reef system, the outermost layer of the reef is the living coral colony. As the reef grows, layers are added. Coral reef growth is extremely slow, taking decades to establish itself. Because of this, efforts must be made to protect coral reef systems and live reefs should not be harvested for the aquarium trade. Dead coral harvested from the shore is perfectly suitable for the aquarium after it has been properly cleaned. I recommend that you boil all coral and other tank decorations collected from the seashore.

If you choose to stock your aquarium with real coral, make sure it comes from a dealer who is a member of the American Marine Dealers Association.

Many aquarium stores carry corals that may have been harvested from living reefs; it is very difficult to determine if the coral has been illegally killed. Dealers who belong to the American Marine Dealers Association (AMDA) carry products that have not been harvested illegally. These conservation-oriented dealers make every effort not to carry fish that are endangered or captured illegally. You should make sure your dealer is a member of the AMDA.

39

The alternative to dead coral is artificial coral replicas. These are becoming increasingly popular and readily available as coral reef protection is increasing worldwide. These natural-looking synthetics are safe for the aquarium and provide the same benefits as real coral, with the exception of water buffering. Many large commercial aquariums utilize artificial coral to mimic the natural reef system. Once the artificial coral is overgrown with algae, it is virtually indistinguishable from the real thing. Most importantly, fish cannot tell the difference.

Most coral that you purchase will be bleached white. In a natural setting and a well balanced aquarium, this will not last. Algal colonization will add green and brown to the coral, diminishing its sterile look. While some beginners find this "dirty" look unappealing, be assured that it is more natural looking. The occasional removal of algae by boiling is recommended if growth becomes excessive and unsightly.

We have all seen beautiful photos of saltwater aquariums teeming with life including live coral. These systems are established by hobbyists who often have years of experience in aquarium keeping. As a novice, don't try to add live coral to your tank. These invertebrate animals have very special needs and can be extremely difficult to maintain in good health.

OTHER ROCK WORK

Other than coral, there are other decorative materials available to the marine aquarist. Tufa is a naturally occurring calcareous rock that is soft and easy to shape. It has all the beneficial attributes of coral including the buffering of water.

Slate is more often used in freshwater aquaria, but also works in the marine tank. Shells are popular natural additions to the saltwater aquarium. Be sure to boil shells before using them in your tank. Sea fans provide "plantlike" decoration to the aquarium, but must be soaked to expose the black skeleton before use.

The use of "living rock" has become popular in the aquarium trade. Live rock is usually a piece of calcerous stone (usually dead coral) harvested from the sea that is covered with multiple forms of living animals and algae, and a number of microorganisms that inhabit the surface of the rock. While live rock is certainly a part of the natural reef ecosystem, like live coral, I do not recommend it for the novice. Keeping these animals alive can be very challenging. Death of any or all of them will sufficiently degrade the water quality of the aquarium, causing trouble for other tank inhabitants. However, healthy live rock can provide excellent biological filtration and a food source for many tank inhabitants.

Pet stores sell a variety of tank decorations that enhance the habitat you are providing your fish. Some come in the forms of plastic or ceramic creations and others are simply well selected rocks and stones. By purchasing these tank decorations from the dealer, you are avoiding the addition of toxic substances and water chemistry modifying agents to your tank. Avoid the temptation to collect your own rocks until you know how to identify each kind and its influence on the water. Before buying any decorations for your aquarium, take the time to design the kind of setting you want to build for your fish. Keep in mind that the natural habitats of fish must provide shelter as well as sufficient swimming space.

Other Accessories

As you develop your talents as an aquarist, you will begin to accumulate many accessories for your tank that make your job easier and help you maintain a happy healthy aquarium. The following are a couple of items that will give you a head start.

I have already mentioned the importance of water quality test kits. Make sure that when you purchase your complete aquarium setup these are not left out. Test kits that measure pH and nitrogen compounds are a must. Included in the latter should be tests for ammonia, nitrite and nitrate.

There are a couple of handy accessories that will help you keep your tank clean. An algal sponge or aquarium cleaner is a sponge attached to a long handle and is used for scraping down the inside of the tank without having to empty the aquarium out. The sponge will easily scrape off algae, but will not scratch the glass. Along these lines, a magnetic aquarium cleaner is also an effective cleaning tool. This involves the use of two magnets bearing cleaning surfaces. One magnet is kept outside the tank and the other is driven on the inside walls of the tank by the outside magnet. An aquarium vacuum is a must for the beginner. This is usually a hand pump siphon that extracts larger debris from the aquarium floor so you don't have to submerse your hands or use a net.

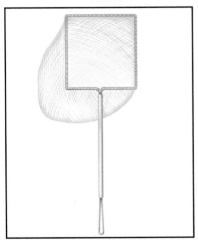

A fishnet will be extremely useful to you as a fish-keeper.

All aquariums should be well equipped to handle fish. This means that you will definitely need a fishnet or two. It's better to have a couple of sizes handy depending on the size of your tank and the size of your fish. Too small a net will be difficult to use to corner a fish and too large a net will be difficult to maneuver in the tank. You will use a fishnet more than you think. It will come in very handy when you need to remove a fish that is ill, dead or aggressive.

There are other items you will use during routine aquarium maintenance that need to be within an arm's length. A 5-gallon bucket and a siphon hose of adequate length are two items which you should commit to use only with your aquarium. This will lessen the need to prepare a clean bucket or hose every time you use one and it will lessen the likelihood of introducing toxic agents into the aquarium each time you use a different bucket or hose.

chapter 3

Setting Up
Your Aquarium

The first step to properly setting up you new aquarium is to assemble all the components in the area where you want the aquarium to be. Once you are confident that everything is in order, take the following steps to set up your aquarium.

McCulloch's Basslet

1. Make sure that everything is clean. Give the gravel, tank, filter, heater, aquarium decorations and anything else you expect to put in the tank a thorough rinsing with clean, warm water. Residues, dirt and other toxic agents can accumulate on your equipment between the time it is manufactured and the time it gets to your home. When it comes to cleaning aquarium decorations like coral and shells, boil them in fresh water. Never use any kind of soap when cleaning your aquarium components; this can cause immediate water quality problems.

Cleaning your gravel is a very important part of this process. Uncleaned gravel will add dust to the aquarium making it cloudy and unhealthy. To clean gravel, empty it into a large container and fill the container with water. Thoroughly agitate the water and stir the gravel before dumping out the water. Do this several times until the water you pour off is clear. For brand new gravel, four to five rinsings is usually sufficient.

2. Place the tank on its stand exactly where you want it to reside. Do not expect to move the tank once it is filled with water. Now you can begin assembling the interior of your aquarium. It is time to aquascape your tank beginning with the lowermost layer, the gravel. Be sure to place your undergravel filter and airlift tubes before gently pouring the gravel into the tank. Terrace the gravel so that it is slightly higher in the back than in the front of the tank. This will add a natural depth of field to your aquarium.

Pour water into the aquarium over a slanted surface to avoid disrupting your aquascape.

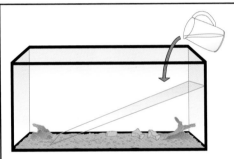

3. Add any larger pieces of coral, rock, etc. Don't attempt to add smaller decorations until the water is added to the tank; they may be disrupted by the filling process. Remember to leave spaces for heaters, filters and other equipment.

4. This would be an appropriate time to add the airstones to the aquarium, taking the opportunity to conceal air supply tubing behind larger decorations.

5. Add water to the tank. To avoid disrupting your aquascape, place a clean plate or bowl on the substrate and pour the water onto it. In most households, tap water will be the appropriate water source. If you suspect that your tap water contains chemical impurities like nitrates, sulphates or phosphates, or is chemically treated with chloramine,

check with your local water company. In these cases, you may need to purchase water or to purify the tap water with deionizers or nitrate-removing resin. In most cases, the aquarium aging process combined with filtration with alleviate minor tap water problems.

Be sure to keep track of the amount of water used to fill the aquarium. Add the artificial salt mix to the aquarium following the manufacturer's instructions for the amount of water you used to fill the tank.

6. Place the heater in the tank and position it. Position the heater in such a way as to maximize its output. Place it near sources of water circulation, like filter outlets or airstones.

   Do not set up the external power filter with activated carbon at this time. Wait until the water has matured before using chemical and mechanical filtration. Also, do not set up the protein skimmer until the tank has matured and is ready for its inhabitants.

7. Place the smaller decorations in the tank, add the thermometer and fine-tune your aquascape.

8. Fit the hood, making sure that the external components and electrical equipment are properly placed. Add the light on top of the canopy and make sure it is correctly hooked up.

9. When you are confident that the electrical wiring is safely insulated from sources of water, plug in the aquarium units and turn on the system. Make sure the heater is properly adjusted; this may take a day or so. Check the operation of the under-gravel filter, air pumps and light.

10. Use the hydrometer to check the specific gravity. If it is a floating hydrometer, use it the following way: First, transfer some aquarium water to a suitable container. This may be the plastic tube that the hydrometer came in. Make sure that there is enough water to float the hydrometer. Then place the hydrometer in the tube, make sure that it is

floating freely, and read the hydrometer at the waterline. This is the specific gravity of the water in your tank. Some authors feel that it is necessary to convert specific gravity to salinity, but this is not required as long as the temperature in your tank is kept relatively constant. If the specific gravity is not ideal, don't add fresh water or additional salt for 24 hours. This allows for all the salt to dissolve and reach an equilibrium. After 24 hours, add more salt if the specific gravity is less than 1.024 or remove water and add tap water if the salinity is greater than 1.024.

11. Let the tank water mature before adding any fish.

Aquarium Maturation

When you have completed the above steps you will have a tank filled with water, but you will not have the working, well balanced artificial habitat for

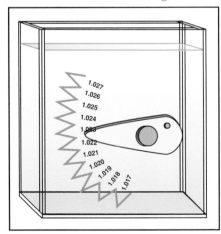

fish that we call an aquarium. To get to this, you need to let the tank mature. Recall that fish require suitable water quality with appropriate levels of water pH, salinity, temperature and biological filtration. Your tap water may harbor treatment additives that can harm your fish. In addition, your new tank does not have a well established nitrogen cycle. These water parameters need to be estab-

Check the salinity of the tank water using a hydrometer.

lished before fish can be added to the tank. Water circulation, temperature regulation and filtration will help your water to mature, but it can take as long as four to five weeks to establish bacterial colonies sufficient to drive the nitrogen cycle.

After your aquarium is set up and the components are turned on, the water maturation process will begin. There are a couple of proven methods for accelerating this process so that fish can be introduced within a couple of weeks. How soon you can introduce your fish depends on how fast ammonia and nitrite levels peak and then drop. One of these methods involves the introduction of commercially prepared maturing fluids and bacterial cultures. Talk to your aquarium dealer to see which product is recommended. By following the manufacturer's instructions,

these preparations will introduce the necessary ingredients to "jump start" the bacterial filter.

Another very effective method involves the incorporation of gravel from an established aquarium into your substrate. After your aquarium is set up and filled with water, go to your local pet store and ask for a handful of gravel from one of their systems that has been well established. Of course, you want to make sure that the store has healthy fish and well maintained aquaria. Mix the gravel in with your gravel. This will accelerate water conditioning by "seeding" the new undergravel filter with bacteria and detritus. A third approach involves the use of live rock to seed a new aquarium. For aforementioned reasons, I only recommend the use of this method if you are guided by an experienced dealer.

> ### BRINGING YOUR FISH HOME
>
> When you bring a fish home, the pet dealer will put it in a plastic bag with water and enough oxygen for a short trip. Ask to have the plastic bag placed inside a dark opaque bag. Keeping the fish in the dark will help reduce the stress of the trip. You must resist the temptation to take the fish out and gawk at it. Bringing the fish from the dark into the light into the dark again can put the fish in shock. Keep it in the bag until you get home.

It is important to test your water daily to determine when the water is properly conditioned and when you can add fish to the tank. In general, once you have seeded the tank with bacteria, the sequence of events will proceed as follows:

1. The amount of ammonia will slowly begin to increase after a few days. As ammonia builds and the bacterial colony grows, the ammonia will be converted to nitrite and this will begin to increase. The pH level will begin to fall as these other parameters rise.

2. As the bacterial population proliferates, ammonia will begin to decline and nitrite will continue to increase; pH should stabilize, but at a level lower than 8.2. This period can take days or weeks depending on the amount of seeding.

3. As ammonia is consumed by bacteria, nitrite will begin to be converted to nitrate, which will slowly rise. Nitrite will peak and suddenly collapse as nitrate continues to rise. At this point, the tank is ready for the introduction of a couple of hardy tank inhabitants. But first, check the pH. The pH may remain low as the tank matures or it may rise as nitrogenous wastes are removed. If the pH is lower than 8.0, correct it after the tank has matured by performing a 50 percent water change. This will also remove nitrate that has accumulated in the aquarium during the conditioning process.

The filter bed will not be completely established for several months, so be sure to be very conservative when you add your first fish. Start with a very low number of peaceful, inexpensive fish. The introduction of very territorial fish like some of the

Take some gravel from an established aquarium and introduce it to your new one. This will speed up the maturation process considerably. (Blue-Spotted Jawfish)

damsels may make it difficult to add more fish, since these fish will establish territories and may be aggressive toward new fish. Closely monitor ammonia and nitrite levels after the first fish are added to make sure that the biological filtration can handle the new load. You can also start your external filter with activated carbon (about 1.5 ounces per 10 gallons of aquarium water) and your protein skimmer at this time.

Placing Fish In the Tank

When you leave your pet store, you will most likely have the fish you selected packed in plastic bags. Make sure the dealer fills the space in the bag with air. Take care not to disturb or shock your fish during transport. Don't expose the bags to excessive changes of temperature or light and don't bounce them around during the trip home. Follow these steps when you get home.

1. Float the plastic bag with fish in your tank so that the temperature in the bag can acclimate to that of the aquarium. Let the bag sit in the tank for at least 10 to 15 minutes.

2. Open the bag and let air in. To insure that the fish will not be shocked by the aquarium water, make sure that both have a temperature within a degree of each other. Add a handful of water from your aquarium to the bag and let it sit for another 10 to 15 minutes.

3. Add the fish to the tank by gently inverting the bag into the tank, letting the fish out.

The first fish you introduce into your tank should be hearty and non-territorial, like this bicolor Blenny.

QUARANTINE TANK

Serious aquarists establish a quarantine tank for new fish to inhabit for a few days to evaluate the health of the fish. A quarantine tank is a much smaller and simpler aquarium set up for that purpose. The quarantine tank needs to be properly filtered and tested routinely, just as the main aquarium. As a beginner, you shouldn't need such a tank if you buy hardy fish from a reputable dealer. Taking care of one tank will probably be enough to start with; two tanks may compound the problems.

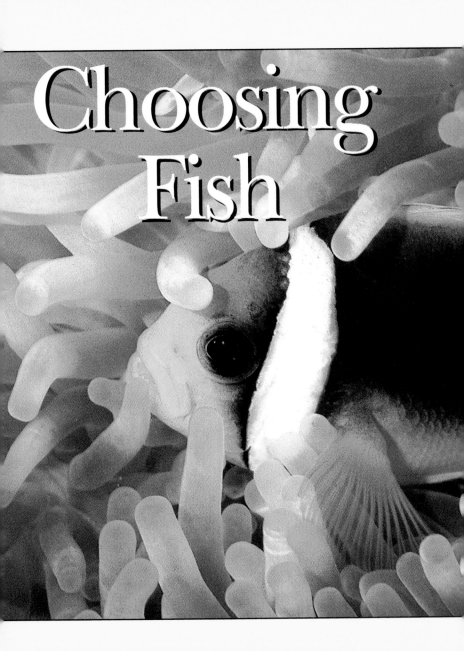

Choosing Fish

for
Beginners

chapter 4

Common Tropical Marine Fish Families

Six-Banded Grouper

The vast majority of marine fish sold by pet dealers originates from warm tropical coral reefs. Their brilliant colors, unique body shapes and animated behavior make these fish preferred saltwater tank inhabitants. The coral reef system is a diverse community of plants (algae), invertebrates and vertebrate animals that function as a whole. The coral reef itself functions as the foundation upon which the community is built.

With this in mind, you are faced with a wide selection of tank inhabitants, both vertebrate, like fish, or invertebrate. There are basically three ways to stock the marine aquarium: the fish-only tank, the invertebrate tank and the mixed fish-invertebrate tank.

Invertebrate animals refer to all those creatures that lack an internal skeleton and a backbone. About 97 percent of all animals in the world are invertebrate. Insects, worms, sponges and snails are a few examples. Vertebrates, on the other hand, have internal skeletons and backbones. Common vertebrates are mammals, reptiles, birds, amphibians and, of course, fish. Marine invertebrates like crabs, snails, coral, anemones and shrimp are more sensitive to water quality than marine fish. They are more difficult to feed and maintain in an aquarium than fish. If you mix them with too many fish, the nitrogenous wastes of the fish will kill them. For these reasons, I thoroughly recommend that the beginner not try to establish an invertebrate or mixed species aquarium until he or she has plenty of experience. The only exception to this would be the introduction of a single anemone to accompany clownfish in an established aquarium.

Invertebrates like this Japanese Anemone Crab and the anemone on which it rests are beautiful, but can be difficult for a beginner to maintain.

In this section, I am going to touch upon the various families of fish that commonly inhabit coral reefs and whose members may be available for your tropical fish-only marine aquarium. By no means is this a complete list of tropical marine fish families, since there are literally thousands of species and hundreds of families. I strongly recommend that you consult the references listed in chapter 11 for more comprehensive information about the species listed below.

SHARKS

There are at least thirty-one families and 350 species of sharks in the world, most of which have never been kept in aquaria. Sharks in general attain sizes too large for the home aquarium, can be very aggressive, and are very sensitive to water quality. For these reasons alone, sharks are not recommended for the beginner.

An anemone to accompany a Clark's Anemonefish is a relatively easy invertebrate addition to the beginner's tank.

MORAY EELS

These well known, unique fish belong to the family Muraenidae. The morays lack pectoral fins, but possess small gill openings and long fanglike teeth. Morays are generally nocturnal fish, feeding on other fish and invertebrates at night and spending most of their daytime hours in holes and crevices. In the wild, these fish easily attain lengths in excess of 5 feet, but this is not common in the average aquarium. Although moray eels will readily accept a variety of foods, they are carnivorous and will consume smaller tankmates. These fish are not recommended for the peaceful community tank.

SQUIRRELFISH

These red fish of the family Holocentridae are normally nocturnal creatures in the wild, using their large eyes to feed at night. In the aquarium, they can be conditioned to feed during the day. Their long bodies have two dorsal fins: a longer fin of spines and a shorter, soft-rayed fin close to the tail. Squirrelfish need a lot of space to accommodate their highly active nature and may be disruptive to a peaceful community tank. In addition, as they get larger, they may consume smaller fish.

SEAHORSES AND PIPEFISH

These exotic fish of the family Syngnathidae are no strangers to the aquarium trade. The pipefish lack the prehensile tail, vertical swimming position and angled head characteristic of the seahorses. Unfortunately, both seahorses and pipefish have feeding and water quality requirements that make it difficult for the beginner to maintain them in the aquarium for any length of time. They do not compete well with other species for food. These fish are very peaceful and do best in a very quiet aquarium. The group is characterized by unusual reproductive behavior in which the female deposits eggs into an abdominal pouch on the male. They are then fertilized and incubated by the male in his pouch.

LIONFISH AND SCORPIONFISH

No aquarium book is complete without mention of these unusual fish of the family Scorpaenidae. This family is comprised of over 300 species of fish with stocky spiny heads and spiny fins armed with venom glands. They are generally predators that hover or lie in wait for prey, suddenly lunging at and engulfing it. Their camouflaged coloration helps them catch their prey successfully. For obvious reasons, these fish must be handled with great care. In captivity, they are generally peaceful but will readily consume smaller tankmates. The novice is best to avoid them.

Seahorses are delicate, peaceful fish and do best in a quiet, non-competitive aquarium.

GRUNTS

These fast growing, hardy fish are so named for the grunting noises they make when their swim bladders amplify the sound generated by the grinding of their teeth. Belonging to the family Haemulidae, the grunts accept a wide variety of foods but require a lot of space. It is best to keep only small juveniles in small schools.

SWEETLIPS

This group of fish was once lumped in the same family as the grunts, but has since been placed in its own family, known as the Plectorhynchidae. Originating in the Indo-Pacific, sweetlips can be active like grunts but are excellent aquarium inhabitants as juveniles. They are generally brightly colored as juveniles, becoming more drab as they get older. These fish have a quiet disposition, preferring a community tank without aggressive tankmates.

SNAPPERS

These fish of the family Lutjanidae, which includes over 200 species, are another group of fast growing, highly active fish that are not suitable as adults for the average marine aquarium. Several species of this family are commercially exploited for food throughout the world. These fish are predatory by nature, require a lot of space and will quickly dominate an aquarium.

GROUPERS AND SEA BASS

Like the grunts and snappers, this group of fish of the family Serranidae is comprised of fast-growing, large predatory fishes. Most, therefore, require larger aquariums if they are to be kept for any length of time. Nonetheless, with over 350 species belonging to this family, there are a few smaller species that are suitable for the peaceful aquarium of the beginner. Many of the groupers are nocturnal, spending most of their day hiding or laying on the bottom.

CARDINALFISH

This group of fish of the family Apogonidae is comprised of almost 200 species of slow-moving, peaceful fish. Large eyes, two separate erect dorsal fins and a large head are characteristic of these fish. Although nocturnal, cardinals can be acclimated to daytime feeding and activity. When kept with other tranquil species in a community tank, these fish are well suited for the beginner.

FAIRY BASSLETS

There are only three species of basslets in the family Grammidae. These somewhat shy fish from the Caribbean prefer a lot of shelter which they will defend from other tank inhabitants. Although a beautiful addition to any tank, the basslet's finicky habits are best suited for the invertebrate tank of the experienced hobbyist.

DOTTYBACKS

These fish of the family Pseudochromidae are very similar to the fairy basslets in size and appearance, yet they are distributed in the Indo-Pacific while the latter are confined to the Caribbean. This family contains the large genus *Pseudochromis* comprised of about forty species. Unfortunately, some of the dottybacks can be highly territorial and care must be taken when choosing the right species for the peaceful marine aquarium.

BUTTERFLYFISH

These are popular aquarium fish belonging to the family Chaetodontidae that have oval flattened bodies, terminal mouths and stunning color patterns. The butterflies are well adapted to life on the coral reef, feeding on the reef itself seeking algae, sponges and corals. Although very beautiful, these fish are very sensitive to water quality changes and are not the hardiest of marine tropicals. Feeding in captivity can be difficult and some species can be territorial. Not recommended for the inexperienced fish hobbyist.

ANGELFISH

The angelfish are often confused with the butterfly-fish because of their ornate colors and deep, flattened bodies. The angels, however, belong to the family Pomacanthidae and can be readily distinguished from the butterflies by the presence of a spine on the gill cover. Angelfish from coral reefs throughout the world are very popular aquarium fish. Some grow quite large (over 24 inches) while others don't grow longer than a few inches. Angels come in a variety of colors and patterns, sometimes changing as the fish matures from juvenile to adult. In general, angelfish can be offered a variety of foods, but large adults can sometimes be finicky preferring sponges and corals. The pygmy angels are well suited for the home aquarium while other species of angelfish grow larger, are prone to being territorial and do better in large public displays.

CLOWNFISH AND DAMSELFISH

These fishes are very popular in the aquarium trade for all levels of experience. Although comprising one family, the Pomacentridae, this group is usually divided into the clownfish and the damselfish. The clownfish are also called anemonefish because in the wild these small ornate fish are able to live unharmed among the stinging tentacles of anemones. The clowns and the anemones live in harmony; it is believed that both the fish and the anemone receive protection from the relationship. This relationship can be mimicked in the aquarium as well, but clownfish do not need anemones to survive in the aquarium.

Damselfish are considered by many to be the hardiest of the marine aquarium species and are, therefore, often the first to be introduced into the new aquarium. These fish, however, can be territorial and aggressive, and, if introduced too early to a new tank they may not be tolerant of new tankmates. Nonetheless, some of the damsels can be exciting additions to your tank, particularly when introduced in shoals.

WRASSES

The family Labridae is comprised of over 500 species all over the world, not only in the tropical waters. This group is quite diverse with its members having a variety of body shapes, behaviors and sizes. Many wrasse species are capable of changing sex as needed for reproductive purposes. Some are substrate burrowers that require sand while others rest in mucus cocoons at night. Some members perform cleaning services similar to those provided by a few species of gobies. The more active species of wrass can be disruptive to the peaceful tank, aggressive toward smaller fishes or too fast growing for the average tank.

Some species of wrasse, like this Clown Wrasse, are ideal additions to the beginner's tank.

BLENNIES

These long slender very active fish belong to the family Blenniidae, which is comprised of about 300 species. They generally eat a variety of foods from algae to flake foods and prefer hiding places like caves and crevices. Most blennies rarely exceed 4 inches in captivity, and many are peaceful additions to the new aquarium.

GOBIES

Somewhat similar in body shape to the blennies, the gobies belong to the family Gobiidae. Gobies have modified pelvic fins that are joined, forming a sucking disk. This family is the largest of the marine fishes with over 1500 species and 200 genera. Some are able to live out of water for extended periods, returning to water to wet their gills. Like the blennies, gobies prefer hiding places and shelters. Some reef-dwelling gobies act as cleaner fish, removing parasites from other reef fishes at specified cleaner stations on the reef. Most gobies are brightly colored, peaceful and relatively small in size, eating a wide variety of foods.

SURGEONFISH AND TANGS

These common aquarium fish belong to the family Acanthuridae. They are characterized by a distinct profile and flattened oval bodies. Their name is derived from the presence of two "scalpel-like" spines at the base of the caudal fin (tail). These are used in defense or during territorial disputes. These schooling fish are algal grazers in the wild as well as in captivity, but can be trained to take other kinds of food as well. In the wild, they will reach sizes in excess of 15 inches, but rarely half this length in captivity, depending on the species.

RABBITFISH

The family Siganidae originates from the Indo-Pacific and contains two genera and about a dozen species. Their flattened oval bodies and small mouths are similar to those of surgeonfish. In the wild, they prefer to browse on algae and other vegetable matter; in the aquarium they can be lured into taking vegetable foods. These fish possess venom glands in their dorsal and anal spines so care must be taken when handling them. Many rabbitfish are fast-growing and require ample swimming space.

TRIGGERFISH

So named for their first dorsal fin which locks into place, the triggers belong to the family Balistidae, which includes over 130 species. These fish can be quite aggressive and possess sharp teeth well suited to feeding on invertebrates in the wild. They readily accept any food in captivity, but their aggressive nature renders many species of triggerfish unsuitable for the beginner. These fish move primarily using their dorsal and anal fins, saving the tail for emergency situations.

Filefish are well suited for a community aquarium, though the beginner may have some trouble getting them to feed in captivity.

FILEFISH

Like their close relatives the triggerfish, filefish, of the family Monocanthidae, have a modified dorsal spine that locks into place. Unlike the triggers, these fish are more peaceful, less active and generally smaller, making them more ideally suited to a tropical-community tank. However, there may be difficulty in getting these fish to feed in captivity since they normally feed on coral and algae.

BOXFISH AND TRUNKFISH

The fish of the family Ostraciidae possess box-shaped bodies covered with bony plates and no pelvic fins. These fish release poisons into the water when threatened and are, therefore, poorly suited for the average aquarium. Boxfish are generally bottomfeeders and can be intolerant of their own kind.

PORCUPINEFISH

These oddities of the marine aquarium belong to the family Diodontidae. These fish have spiny scales and are able to inflate their bodies to ward off danger. Although relatively easy to keep in captivity, they generally get too large for the average aquarist.

PUFFERS

These fish look like porcupinefish without spines, but they belong to a different family—Tetraodontidae. They are smaller than the porcupines and have fused beaklike jaws. These fish will also inflate to avoid being eaten. Their flesh is poisonous when consumed. These fish are vigorous feeders in the aquarium, but some species can be aggressive.

chapter 5

The Best
(and Worst)
Aquarium Fish
For Beginners

Throughout this book, I have referred to your aquarium as a community tank. The community tank contains different species of compatible fish, while a species tank contains only a single species. I feel that the beginner should establish a community tank to start with because fish of  the community tank are relatively hardy and get along with each other. The species tank concept is best for those who want to maintain fish that require special tank conditions or are extremely aggressive, or for those who want to mix fish with invertebrates.

A wide variety of fish are well suited to the community aquarium. The important thing is to balance the types of fish in your tank. You will recall that species of fish have adapted to varying lifestyles and different behaviors. Some fish will live throughout the tank, while others will stay mainly in the middle or bottom levels. In the community

63

Choosing Fish
for Beginners

tank, you want to recreate this kind of environment by having fish spread throughout the tank, minimizing competition and utilizing the entire aquarium.

In addition, many species of fish school by nature. This can be a very attractive addition to the community tank. These schooling fish should never be kept alone but instead in a group of at least five or six individuals.

From the general overview I presented earlier, you can see that some fish tend to be territorial or aggressive. These should be avoided by the beginner because a single aggressive fish in a community tank can wreak havoc on the other species.

Another aspect of choosing fish that the novice will sometimes overlook is the maximum size of a particular species. Some species grow faster than others. You don't want to put a fish in your tank that will attain a length of 12 inches in less than a year. This will not only disrupt your aquarium capacity, but the larger fish will undoubtedly dominate the tank. Some species are very compatible with other species when they are juveniles, but become solitary and aggressive as adults. These fish do not belong in the peaceful community tank.

When your tank is fully established, the water chemistry has balanced, and you are ready to stock your aquarium, I thoroughly recommend that you have a game plan in mind. Don't blindly go to your pet dealer and look for fish for your tank. This can result in fish incompatibility. Instead, determine beforehand the kind of fish you want to start with. Take some of my suggestions in this section. Consult with some of the fish encyclopedias listed in the final section of this book. In other words, establish a list of potential fish that you want to introduce into your aquarium. Remember to choose a variety of species that will live throughout the water column from the top to the bottom.

Tropical marine fish are more expensive than their freshwater counterparts and most are taken from reefs around the world and not bred in captivity. Therefore, be selective when you get to the pet store. Buy fish only from healthy looking aquariums with clear water, clean panes, and no dead fish in the tank. Make sure that the fish you want is healthy looking. If the fish has any cuts, scrapes or fin problems, don't buy it. Watch for possible symptoms of disease such as white granular spots, cottony white patches, frayed fins or dull skin. Watch the behavior of the fish. Healthy fish swim in a lively manner and are not shy.

You may even want to see the fish feed before you buy it to make sure that it has recovered from the stress of shipping and has acclimated to life in an aquarium.

Many feel that it is important to introduce your fish to the aquarium in batches, buying fish in lots every few weeks to a month. This is important for the newly established aquarium. This allows fish to acclimate to each other and prevents aggressive behavior towards a single fish when it is introduced. Be sure not to stock a marine aquarium too rapidly and follow the tank capacity guidelines outlined earlier.

Flamefish.

The following is a list of tropical marine species that are relatively easy to take care of. They are well suited for the beginner's community tank where pH ranges from 8.1 to 8.3 and temperature is maintained between 75 and 79 degrees F. I have listed both the common and scientific names and have tried to include common representatives of each of the groups reviewed above. Also included is information on which level of the tank the fish is most likely to inhabit. The sizes listed below are those attained in captivity, which are generally less than in the wild.

Flamefish *(Apogon maculatus)*

Family: Apogonidae
Distribution: Western Atlantic
Size: 3 inches
Food: Omnivorous
Tank Level: Middle and Lower Levels

The Flamefish is one of the tranquil cardinalfish that is well suited for the beginner's aquarium. This fish has a striking red coloration, prefers a peaceful aquarium and takes all kinds of aquarium foods that will fit into its mouth. Since cardinalfish are nocturnal by nature, they may be a bit shy at first and it is best to feed these fish in the evening.

*Pajama
Cardinalfish.*

Pajama Cardinalfish *(Sphaeramia nematopterus)*

Family: Apogonidae
Distribution: Indo-Pacific
Size: 3 inches
Food: Omnivorous
Tank Level: Middle and Lower Levels

This species of cardinalfish has three distinct color patterns on its body, each completely different. Like other cardinalfish, the Pajama has large eyes for nocturnal feeding and it can be kept in groups. Care must be taken not to introduce boisterous fish with cardinalfish because this will disrupt their quiet lifestyle.

Strawberry Gramma (*Pseudochromis porphyreus*)

Family: Pseudochromidae
Distribution: Central and Western Pacific
Size: 2 inches
Food: Omnivorous
Tank Level: Lower Levels

Strawberry Gramma.

The Strawberry Gramma is a brilliant purple dottyback that is very easy to feed and very hardy in captivity. Like many dottybacks, however, it can be aggressive toward similar species or similar-looking species. Therefore, it is best kept singly. It will accept most marine frozen, live and flake foods. Similar species: Flash-Back Gramma *(Pseudochromis diadema)*.

Threadfin Butterflyfish.

Threadfin Butterflyfish (*Chaetodon auriga*)

Family: Chaetodontidae
Distribution: Indo-Pacific, Red Sea
Size: 4 inches

Food: Omnivorous
Tank Level: Middle and Lower Levels

The butterflyfish in general are not suitable for the inexperienced aquarist because they can be difficult to keep. However, a couple of species are very popular in the aquarium trade and can fare quite well if water quality is properly maintained. The Threadfin is named for the threadlike extension that develops on the dorsal fin of the adults. It will consume a variety of aquarium foods and particularly enjoys live brine shrimp. Similar species: Vagabond Butterflyfish *(Chaetodon vagabundus)*, Klein's Butterflyfish *(Chaetodon kleini)*, Raccoon Butterflyfish *(Chaetodon lunula)*.

Wimplefish.

Wimplefish *(Heniochus acuminatus)*
Family: Chaetodontidae
Distribution: Indo-Pacific, Red Sea
Size: 6 inches
Food: Omnivorous
Tank Level: Middle and Lower Levels

This peaceful butterflyfish is easy to keep and easy to feed and may be kept in groups of two or three if your aquarium is large enough. On the Wimplefish, the front rays of the dorsal fin are extended and grow with age. Young of this species have been known to act as cleaner fish.

Dwarf Angelfish (*Centropyge* species)

Family: Pomacanthidae
Distribution: Atlantic, Pacific, Indian
Size: 3 inches
Food: Omnivorous
Tank Level: All Levels

As stated earlier, angelfish in general can grow to large sizes and have a tendency to become aggressive and territorial as they get older. Unless you plan on maintaining large boisterous fish in a high capacity aquarium, the Dwarf Angelfish of the genus *Centropyge* are colorful and peaceful angelfish for the beginner. Specifically, this group includes: the African Pygmy Angel *(C. acanthops)*, the Coral Beauty *(C. bispinosus)*, the Lemonpeel Angel *(C. flavissimus)*, Herald's Angel *(C. heraldi)*, the Flame Angel *(C. loriculus)*, the Resplendent Angel *(C. resplendens)* and the Cherubfish *(C. argi)*. Unlike the larger species of angelfish, many of these angels associate in pairs and can be kept with members of the same species. These fish enjoy a variety of marine foods. An added advantage of these angelfish is that they are compatible with many marine invertebrates should you decide to diversify in the future. It is important to provide a lot of aquarium decorations for these species to seek refuge in.

Common Clownfish (*Amphiprion ocellaris*)

Family: Pomocentridae
Distribution: Indo-Pacific

*Common
Clownfish.*

Size: 2 inches
Food: Omnivorous
Tank Level: Middle and Lower Levels

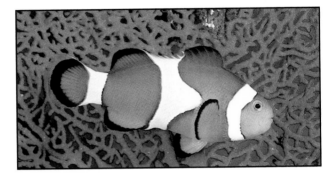

The Common Clownfish is the most popular anemone-fish in the aquarium trade. This species does not do well singly and should be maintained in pairs. It feeds well on a variety of finely chopped frozen foods and can be coaxed into accepting flake. These fish do best, however, when kept with an anemone. The ambitious beginner should avoid these fish until several months of experience are attained and the quality of the aquarium has stabilized.

Clark's Anemonefish
(*Amphiprion clarki*)
Family: Pomocentridae
Distribution: Indo-Pacific
Size: 3 inches
Food: Omnivorous
Tank Level: Middle and
Lower Levels

These hardy, peaceful community fish can live happily without an anemone, but more than one may not get along. Their coloration can vary according to locality of capture. This fish will eat a variety of foods including flake, live foods and green foods. Similar species: Tomato Clownfish (*Amphiprion frenatus*).

*Clark's
Anemonefish.*

Sergeant Major *(Abudefduf saxatilis)*

Family: Pomocentridae
Distribution: Indo-Pacific, Atlantic
Size: 2 inches
Food: Omnivorous
Tank Level: All Levels

Sergeant Major.

This black-banded damselfish is a very active shoaling species that should be kept in groups of four or more. It is considered an ideal marine tropical for the beginner because it is hardy and accepts a wide variety of marine foods. In addition, the Sergeant Major is less territorial and pugnacious than other damsels. Note that other damsels including the Blue Damselfish *(Abudefdul cyaneus)*, the Humbud Damselfish *(Dascyllus carneus)*, the Yellow-tailed Damselfish *(Chromis xanthurus)* and the Beau Gregory *(Stegastes leucostictus)* are also considered excellent fish for the beginner because they are extremely hardy and easy to feed. However, these fish can be territorial as well, creating problems for the other occupants of your tank.

Green Chromis *(Chromis viridis)*

Family: Pomocentridae
Distribution: Indo-Pacific, Red Sea
Size: 2 inches
Food: Omnivorous
Tank Level: Middle Levels

This is another peaceful, colorful damselfish that should be kept in a shoal of six or more. The Green

Green Chromis.

Chromis is an active fish that may be finicky to start, but will consume a variety of chopped meaty foods after it has acclimated to the aquarium.

Spanish Hogfish (*Bodianus rufus*)
Family: Labridae
Distribution: Western Atlantic
Size: 8 inches
Food: Omnivorous
Tank Level: All levels

*Spanish
Hogfish.*

Many of the wrasse grow quite large and this must be taken into account when one is purchased. In general, juveniles are very peaceful, hardy fish that accept a variety of marine foods. Young Spanish Hogfish are known to service other fish as cleaners. As the fish matures the coloration changes with red becoming more predominant, though this will vary depending on locality of capture. Larger hogfish will make a meal of smaller aquarium inhabitants, so you may need to remove them once they grow too large. Similar species: Cuban Hogfish *(Bodianus pulchellus).*

African Clown Wrasse *(Coris formosa)*

Family: Labridae
Distribution: Indo-Pacific, Red Sea
Size: 8 inches
Food: Carnivorous
Tank Level: Lower Level

African Clown Wrasse.

This wrasse also changes colors as it matures; its white stripes change to blue-green. This bottom-feeder prefers live marine invertebrates like brine shrimp as well as other meaty foods. It is best to keep it as a single specimen in your tank, since there is a tendency for them to quarrel among themselves. The African Clown Wrasse is generally safe with small fishes as a juvenile, but this may change as they get older. Similar species: Clown Wrasse *(Coris gaimardi)*.

Cleaner Wrasse servicing Blue-faced Tilefish.

Cleaner Wrasse *(Labroides dimidiatus)*

Family: Labridae
Distribution: Indo-Pacific
Size: 2 inches

Food: Carnivorous
Tank Level: All Levels

The Cleaner Wrasse is a very popular fish in the marine aquarium and a must for the beginner. As the name implies, this fish is indispensable at feeding on the parasites of other tank inhabitants, working around the body, gills and mouth of its client. The fish not only provides a useful service for the tank but also feeds in a natural manner. Meaty marine foods can augment the fish's diet. More than one cleaner can be kept in the same tank. Similar species: *Labroides phthirophagus.*

Four-spot Wrasse.

Four-spot Wrasse *(Halichoeres trispilus)*
Family: Labridae
Distribution: Indian Ocean
Size: 4 inches
Food: Carnivorous
Tank Level: All Levels

With its bright yellow body and characteristic four black spots, this wrasse is a beautiful addition to the beginner's aquarium. It's a hardy, peaceful fish that readily accepts a variety of frozen and live marine foods. Similar species: Banana Wrasse *(Halichoeres chrysus)*.

Yellow Sweetlips *(Plectorhynchus albovittatus)*
Family: Plectorhynchidae
Distribution: Indo-Pacific, Red Sea
Size: 4 inches
Food: Carnivorous
Tank Level: Middle and Lower Levels

In general, the sweetlips are hardy but shy fishes that feed on meaty marine foods. The colors on these fish change with age. The beautiful yellow stripes of the yellow sweetlips fade, and the fish become more brown as they get larger. This species can be reclusive if kept with boisterous tankmates but is ideal for a peaceful tank.

*Yellow
Sweetlips.*

Midas Blenny *(Ecsenius midas)*
Family: Blenniidae
Distribution: Indian Ocean, Red Sea
Size: 3 inches
Food: Omnivorous
Tank Level: Lower Level

Midas Blenny.

Like most blennies, this fish needs plenty of nooks and caves to hide in. Once acclimated, the Midas Blenny is quite animated, perching itself on rocks to observe the rest of the aquarium. This yellow-hued fish swims like an eel, and its healthy appetite for all types of food makes it an ideal beginner's fish.

Bicolor Blenny *(Ecsenius bicolor)*
Family: Blenniidae
Distribution: Indo-Pacific
Size: 3 inches
Food: Omnivorous
Tank Level: Lower Level

Bicolor Blenny.

This blenny has a front half that is brown and a rear half that is orange, hence the name. The Bicolor is a shy species of fish that lives in small holes and caves. It too is a pleasure to watch. When feeding, it darts from its home to catch food, quickly returning to the safety of its den by backing in. Like the Midas Blenny, the Bicolor will readily accept a variety of foods.

Lemon Goby.

Lemon Goby *(Gobiodon citrinus)*
Family: Gobiidae
Distribution: Indo-Pacific
Size: 1.5 inches
Food: Carnivorous

Tank Level: Lower Level

The Lemon Goby is a typical goby in that it spends much of its time perched on aquarium decorations quietly observing the rest of the tank. Its coloration—beautiful yellow with blue streaks—is a nice addition to any tank. This is a very peaceful fish that should not be kept with large fish because of its size. Once settled, the Lemon Goby will accept most food but has a particular fondness for live brine shrimp.

Neon Goby.

Neon Goby *(Gobiosoma oceanops)*
Family: Gobiidae
Distribution: Western Atlantic
Size: 1 inch
Food: Omnivorous
Tank Level: Lower Level

This goby is well known for the cleaning services it offers to its tankmates. This popular aquarium fish can be kept in a shoal of five or six as long as no larger predators are present. The Neon Goby is one of the few marine aquarium fish that has been bred in captivity. Unfortunately, it usually only lives between one and two years in the average aquarium.

Orange-spotted Goby *(Valenciennea puellaris)*
Family: Gobiidae
Distribution: Indo-Pacific
Size: 4 inches
Food: Omnivorous
Tank Level: Lower Level

The Orange-spotted Goby is a hardy, colorful fish that will readily accept a variety of suitably sized foods including frozen and flake foods. This species likes to dig into the substrate so a sandy bottom is required.

*Orange-spotted
Goby.*

Blue-cheek Goby *(Valenciennea strigata)*
Family: Gobiidae
Distribution: Western Pacific, Indian Ocean
Size: 3 inches
Food: Omnivorous
Tank Level: Lower Levels

*Blue-cheek
Goby.*

This is an easy-to-keep peaceful goby that will spend much of its time sifting through the substrate for food. This will enhance your filter bed by keeping it free of detritus. The Blue-cheek does well with members of its own kind and can be kept in pairs. This colorful addition to the aquarium thrives on all kind of marine foods.

Goldrim Tang *(Acanthurus glaucopareius)*

Family: Acanthuridae
Distribution: Pacific and Indian Oceans
Size: 6 inches
Food: Herbivorous
Tank Level: All Levels

Goldrim Tang.

The Goldrim's oval body and steeply sloping fore-head is typical of the tangs. This species, like other tangs, prefers a vegetarian diet, so tank algae and vegetables are a must. This species is safe with small fish but is best kept as a single specimen in a large aquarium.

Lipstick Tang.

Lipstick Tang *(Naso lituratus)*

Family: Acanthuridae
Distribution: Indo-Pacific

Size: 8 inches
Food: Herbivorous
Tank Level: All Levels

This species is another peaceful tang that is an attractive addition to the larger aquarium. The common name refers to the red around the mouth of this fish. Remember that tangs have two scalpels on each side of the tail, so care must be taken when handling these fish. Although the Lipstick Tang and other tangs are listed as herbivorous, they can be acclimated to other protein and flake foods.

Regal Tang.

Regal Tang *(Paracanthus hepatus)*
Family: Acanthuridae
Distribution: Indo-Pacific
Size: 6 inches
Food: Herbivorous
Tank Level: All Levels

The deep royal blue and bright yellow tail of this tang is very distinctive and has made this fish a popular aquarium choice. Unfortunately, some of this coloring is lost as the fish gets older. Although some feel that the Regal can be kept with members of the same species, it is best to limit your tank to one unless you have a very large tank. These vegetarians will also accept food like brine shrimp most of the time.

Foxface *(Lo vulpinus)*

Family: Siganidae
Distribution: Pacific
Size: 6 inches
Food: Omnivorous
Tank Level: Middle and Lower Levels

Foxface.

This is the most common rabbitfish kept in captivity. It is sometimes called the Badgerfish because of its facial markings, which highly contrast its bright yellow body. This fish is an algae eater so an aquarium with lush algal growth is preferred. It will, however, accept a variety of foods as long as vegetable matter is presented. The Foxface can be aggressive toward its own kind, so it should be kept singly.

Black-finned Triggerfish.

Black-finned Triggerfish *(Xanichthys ringens)*

Family: Balistidae
Distribution: Indo-Pacific

Size: 10 inches
Food: Omnivorous
Tank Level: All Levels

This is one of the few species of triggerfish recommended for inclusion in a peaceful community tank.
The Black-finned Triggerfish is a gentle fish that readily
accepts all kinds of foods that are offered. It is generally safe with small fishes and is considered to be relatively easy to keep in captivity. It may, however, be
difficult to obtain.

Wreckfish *(Anthias squamipinnis)*
Family: Serranidae
Distribution: Indo-Pacific
Size: 4 inches
Food: Carnivorous
Tank Level: All Levels

Wreckfish.

Belonging to the family of sea basses, the wreckfish is
unlike many of its relatives in that it is a shoaling
species that does not become overly large and predatory. It is best kept in shoals of six or more and adapts
well to a peaceful community tank. It is carnivorous, so
it requires live or meaty foods. A shoal of these colorful fish is a very attractive addition to the aquarium.

Sharp-nosed Puffer *(Canthigaster solandri)*
Family: Tetraodontidae
Distribution: Indo-Pacific, Red Sea

Size: 2 inches
Food: Carnivorous
Tank Level: Middle and Lower Levels

This pufferfish is the smallest and most beautiful of common pufferfish. This species differs from the others in that it is a small species that will not outgrow the tank. It is a peaceful fish that should be kept away from its own kind and it will accept a variety of finely chopped seafood.

Fish to Avoid as Beginners

There are many species of fish that are not well suited for the beginner's aquarium for a number of reasons. Some may be highly sensitive to fluctuating water quality conditions characteristic of the new aquarium. Others may require special water conditions like brackish water. The beginner should not try to provide this type of habitat without acquiring some experience. There are also a number of species that are not socially compatible with the peaceful community tank. This group includes large carnivorous fish that eat smaller fish, territorial fish that do not tolerate trespassing and mature fish that display aggression and combative behavior. Lastly, there are also species of marine fish that exude poison when threatened. In a closed aquarium, this can have deadly consequences.

83

Many of the aggressive species are offered in the pet store and may even be promoted by pet dealers because the fish are smaller juveniles that they consider "harmless." Don't be fooled by this argument; large predatory fish generally grow fast and develop aggressive behavior early in life.

And don't be fooled into buying fish that require special water conditions. These fish may live for days or weeks in your tank, but chronic stress will set in, their immune responses will fail, and they will ultimately die.

As you develop your talents as an aquarist, you will expand your capabilities and be able to keep some of the more sensitive species of fish. You may even want to establish an aquarium of "compatible" aggressive species or a species tank. However, at the early stages of your aquarium keeping career, it is best to concentrate on maintaining water quality with a few compatible and rugged species of fish.

The following is a list of those species to avoid in your tropical community aquarium. These fish are those that you are most likely to encounter in the aquarium store; they are arranged by family.

*Snowflake
Moray.*

MORAY EELS

84

Snowflake Moray *(Echnida nebulosa)*: Large, predatory.

Reticulated Moray *(Gymnothorax favagineus)*: Large, predatory.

SEAHORSES/ PIPEFISH

Banded Pipefish *(Doryrhamphos dactyliophorus)*: Delicate.

Florida Seahorse *(Hippocampus erectus)*: Delicate.

Yellow Seahorse *(Hippocampus kuda)*: Delicate.

Turkeyfish *(Dendrochirus brachypterus)*: Predatory.

Lionfish *(Pterois* species)*: Predatory.

SEA BASS

Marine Betta *(Calloplesiops altivelis)*: Predatory.

Coral Trout *(Cephalopholis miniatus)*: Large, predatory.

Golden-stripe Grouper *(Grammistes sexlineatus)*: Large, predatory.

SNAPPERS

Emperor Snapper *(Lutjanus sebae)*: Grows too large.

Squirrelfish.

SQUIRRELFISH

Common Squirrelfish *(Sargocentron diadema)*: Predatory, boisterous.

85

Fairy Basslets

Black-cap Gramma *(Gramma melacara)*: Highly territorial.

Royal Gramma *(Gramma loreto)*: Highly territorial.

Dottybacks

False Gramma *(Pseudochromis paccagnellae)*: Can be aggressive.

Butterflyfish

Yellow Long-nosed Butterflyfish *(Forcipiger flavissimus)*: Delicate, needs perfect water quality.

Pakistani Butterflyfish *(Chaetodon collare)*: Difficult to feed.

Saddleback Butterflyfish *(Chaetodon ephipippium)*: Difficult to feed, incompatible with others.

Banded Butterflyfish *(Chaetodon striatus)*: Delicate, incompatible.

Copper-band Butterflyfish *(Chelmon rostratus)*: Delicate, difficult to feed, needs very high water quality.

Four-eyed Butterflyfish *(Chaetodon capistratus)*: Delicate.

Red-headed Butterflyfish *(Chaetodon larvatus)*: Delicate.

Chevron Butterflyfish *(Chaetodon trifascialis)*: Delicate.

Angelfish

Three-spot Angelfish *(Apolemichthys trimaculatus)*: Delicate, territorial, difficult to acclimate.

Purple-moon Angelfish *(Arusetta asfur)*: Aggressive, territorial.

Bicolor Cherub *(Centropyge bicolor)*: Delicate.

Blue-faced Angelfish *(Euxiphipops xanthometapon)*: Delicate.

Queen Angelfish *(Holocanthus bermudensis)*: Aggressive, territorial, grows large.

King Angelfish *(Holocanthus passer)*: Very aggressive, grows large.

Rock Beauty *(Holocanthus tricolor)*: Very aggressive, finicky.

French Angelfish *(Pomacanthus paru)*: Grows large.

Koran Angelfish *(Pomacanthus semicirculatus)*: Grows large, territorial.

Regal Angelfish *(Pygoplites diacanthus)*: Delicate, difficult to acclimate.

DAMSELFISH
Blue Devil *(Pomacentrus coeruleus)*: Aggressive.

WRASSES
Dwarf Parrot Wrasse *(Cirrhilabrus rubriventralis)*: Delicate.

Twin-spot Wrasse *(Coris angulata)*: Grows too large.

Harlequin Tuskfish *(Lienardella fasciata)*: Large, predatory.

Moon Wrasse *(Choerodon lunare)*: Boisterous, large, aggressive.

BLENNIES
False Cleanerfish *(Aspidontus taeniatus)*: Predatory fish, biter.

Redlip Blenny *(Ophioblennius atlanticus)*: Territorial.

SURGEONS AND TANGS
Achilles Tang *(Acanthurus achilles)*: Delicate, Not compatible.

Blue Tang *(Acanthurus coeruleus)*: Aggressive as juveniles.

Yellow Tang *(Zebrasoma flavescens)*: Highly territorial.

Blue Tang.

TRIGGERFISH

Undulate Triggerfish *(Balistapus undulatus)*: Large and very aggressive.

White-lined Triggerfish *(Sufflamer bursa)*: Aggressive.

Queen Triggerfish *(Balistes vetula)*: Large predator.

Clown Triggerfish *(Balistoides conspicillum)*: Large predator.

FILEFISH

Long-nosed Filefish *(Oxymonocanthus longirostris)*: Delicate.

PORCUPINEFISH

Spiny Boxfish *(Chilomycterus schoepfi)*: Large, predatory.

Long-spined Porcupinefish *(Diodon holacanthus)*: Large, predatory.

Common Porcupinefish *(Diodon hystrix)*: Large, messy eater.

BOXFISH

Spotted Boxfish *(Ostracion meleagris)*: Poison secreting, delicate.

PUFFERFISH

Spotted Puffer *(Arothron meleagris)*: Large, messy eater.

Caring
for Your

part three

Fish

chapter 6

Feeding
Your
Fish

The raw materials needed for life and growth are called nutrients. Fish, like all other animals, need these nutrients for sustenance, growth and reproduction. They can only get these nutrients by eating plants or other animals.

There are many things to take into account when it comes to providing food for your fish. In their natural habitat, fish have evolved various feeding strategies to optimize their ability to get nutrients. With all the different kinds of fish and habitats, you can imagine the many kinds of feeding strategies that exist. In general, fish can be divided into three general groups based on the type of feeding strategy that they have evolved.

Carnivores   In the wild, these fish are primarily predators that feed on fish or invertebrates that they bite, engulf or crush.

Carnivores eat a variety of animals ranging from tiny plankton to large species of fish. When kept in the aquarium, many tropical marine fish have been successfully fed dead food, commercially prepared pellets and flakes or live critters. Pieces of fish, shrimp and other meats will be taken by the carnivore. Some species will simply not accept anything but live food. Guppies, goldfish and brine shrimp are commonly offered to these predators.

Carnivorous fish like this Horn Shark may need to be fed live food, like guppies, goldfish and brine shrimp.

Herbivores   As the name implies, these fish feed on plant matter, mainly algae. Very few tropical marine species are exclusively herbivorous, deriving all their nutrients from plants. From a practical standpoint, there are no strictly herbivorous marine fish in captivity. Studies have shown that all marine aquarium fish known to feed exclusively on plants in the wild will accept animal tissue in captivity. However, it is important to have a lush growth of algae in your aquarium if you intend to house herbivorous fish. You can also augment their diet with household vegetables like blanched lettuce and spinach.

Omnivores   These fish will feed on a variety of foods and have no specific dietary preferences. You have probably noticed that many of the recommended species outlined in chapter 5 are omnivorous. The beginning aquarist should not have to worry about special feeding strategies when setting up a saltwater tank for the first time. Omnivorous fish will accept commercially prepared flake and pellet foods, but providing a good variety of foods is necessary to meet all the dietary requirements of these fish.

Dietary Needs

Like all living animals, fish have dietary requirements for protein, fat, carbohydrates, vitamins and minerals. In their natural environment, fish will meet their own needs by foraging for whatever their body requires. In the home aquarium, fish rely entirely on you to meet their dietary needs. Unfortunately, the nutritional needs of tropical marine fish are very poorly understood. The nutritional requirements of fish differ by species, age, water temperature and many other factors. The best that any aquarist, including the professionals, can do is feed the fish a variety of foods to approximate their requirements.

Fish need a full nutritional complement to remain active and healthy. (Blue Moon Angelfish).

There are many different types of food for your tropical marine fish. Carnivores will eat flake food, brine shrimp and almost any kind of seafood—crab, lobster, oysters and clams. Herbivores will adapt to an omnivorous life taking flake and frozen foods and vegetables, while grazing on aquarium algae. The omnivore will eat all these foods.

FOOD CATEGORIES

Aquarium foods can be grouped several ways into a variety of categories. For marine tropicals, I prefer to classify aquarium foods into three general categories: natural foods, prepared foods and live foods.

The following is a brief description of each category.

Natural Foods

This category of tropical fish food includes items that are obtained fresh, frozen or freeze-dried. These are typically leafy green vegetables, fish and invertebrate flesh and thawed or freeze-dried brine shrimp and other plankton.

Leafy Green Vegetables   It is essential to provide vegetable matter in the diet because some marine species are naturally herbivorous. This can be provided by the algae in your aquarium for grazing fish. You can also feed a variety of vegetables fresh, blanched or thawed including lettuce, spinach, cabbage, parsley, kale and watercress. Some experts recommend blanching the vegetables to aid digestion. In general, vegetables are composed mostly of water and are low in energy, protein and lipid but contain high concentrations of carbohydrate, fiber and certain vitamins. You do not want to feed your fish exclusively vegetables.

Fish and Invertebrate Flesh   This category includes a variety of seafood that is fed fresh, thawed or cooked. Cooking these foods does not lower their nutritional value, and it is a good idea to do so because raw seafood can carry infectious diseases to your fish. You can boil, steam the food or serve foods canned in water (not oil). You generally want to stick to seafood with marine fish because you will be serving your fish foods that have similar composition to themselves. The variety of meats available is vast and can include fish like herring, anchovy, smelt, mackerel and tuna; shellfish like clams, shrimp, mussels, scallops, oysters, crabs and squid. Meaty foods tend to contain less water and carbohydrates and substantially more protein and lipids than vegetable matter. This is a must for carnivorous fish.

Frozen and Freeze-dried Foods   These foods often constitute the greatest portion of your fish's diet because many are specifically processed for aquarium use and are widely available. Some of the most common commercially available frozen foods in this category include brine shrimp, krill and other shrimps. Most commercial processors treat these with gamma rays to ensure that they are disease free. They will keep for several months and can be thawed as needed. The dietary value of this food is similar to that of meaty food.

Freeze-drying has made it possible to preserve a variety of natural foods for aquarium fish. For the marine aquarium, the process has most often been applied to brine shrimp and other small invertebrates like krill. These will help to increase the variety of food you are feeding your fish, but they should not be the only food offered. While it has been shown that freeze-dried brine shrimp have the same lipid concentrations as freshly killed brine shrimp, it has not been proven that they are a complete dietary substitute for live brine shrimp.

FEEDING STRATEGIES

You can divide fish into three groups based on the kind of feeding strategy they use: carnivores, herbivores and omnivores. Carnivores only eat other fish and live food. Herbivores eat only vegetable matter. They will eat flake foods and other types of plant matter. Most of the fish listed in this book are omnivores. They will eat flakes, live foods and bits of table food. Basically, they will eat almost anything. They are clearly the easiest group to feed and are thus the most highly recommended for the beginning aquarist.

Prepared Foods

This category of food contains the commercially processed flake and dried food for aquarium fish. Commercially prepared foods try to approximate the three basic requirements of proteins, fats and carbohydrates. They are also supplemented with vitamins and minerals. These foods come in many varieties depending on the type of fish (carnivore, herbivore, omnivore). New formulations are being added every year to better meet the dietary needs of your fish.

Prepared foods come in many forms depending on the size and feeding behavior of the fish. Flakes, tablets, pellets and crumb forms are available. For example, larger predatory fishes should be fed pellets as opposed to flakes because they prefer to consume a large quantity. In addition, fish that feed on the bottom may not venture to the surface for flakes, so they must be fed pellets or tablets that sink to the bottom. Pellets can be stuck to the aquarium glass for the grazing species in your tank.

Many of the community fish reviewed in this book can be fed prepared foods. However, if you want active, colorful, healthy fish, you must vary their diets. Flakes are best as a staple food, but you should make every effort to substitute other foods daily to enrich your fish.

Live Foods

Live food is an excellent source of nutrition for the tropical marine aquarium. Fish fed live foods ordinarily grow faster and have higher survival rates. This is because live foods retain active enzymes that make digestion more efficient. Many aquarists feel that live foods are an essential requirement of captive fish and should be fed at least as a dietary supplement. The kind of live food you offer will depend on the size of the fish that you are feeding. Small fish like freshwater guppies and goldfish are often fed to large predatory fish like lionfish. By far the most popular live food for the tropical marine fish is brine shrimp.

If you want healthy, active, colorful fish, make an effort to offer a variety of foods. (Coral Beauty)

Brine Shrimp   The brine shrimp (*Artemia* species) is a primitive crustacean inhabiting salt pans in 164 locations around the world. Those in your local pet store probably originated in San Francisco Bay or Great Salt Bay in Utah. They are one of the best sources of nutrition available for fish of any type. They are an excellent source of lipids and protein. Of all the live food available, they are the safest because they do not carry disease. An added advantage to brine shrimp is that you can raise them yourself.

To raise brine shrimp, it is best to follow the instructions accompanying the eggs.

How To Feed Your Fish

The biggest problem when feeding your fish is determining how much and how often to feed them. Some fish are gluttons while others will stop when they are sated. It is definitely better to feed too little than too much to your fish. Follow the guidelines below when feeding your fish and you will develop a working sense of how much and how often to feed.

1. Offer as much food as your fish will eat in five minutes. Flakes should sink no deeper than one-third the height of the tank; provide tablets or pellets for bottom fish.

2. Feed your fish in very small portions over the five-minute period.

3. If you are home during the day, feed your fish over the course of the day in small portions. If you are not home, feed you fish twice a day at the same times every day, once in the morning, once at night.

4. Always feed your fish at the same spot in the tank.

5. Don't overfeed the fish, no matter how much you think they need more food. Overeating will stress your fish and cause detritus to accumulate in the tank, degrading water quality.

Watch all your fish during feeding, making sure that each gets its share of food. Remember that fish have different mouth shapes that allow them to feed at different levels in the tank. Some species will not go to the surface to eat and will wait for food to disperse throughout the tank. Don't rely on surface feedings and the leftovers of others to feed bottom fish. Pellets or other foods that sink to the bottom should be provided to these fish. Remember, refusal to eat is one of the first signs of illness, so keep an eye out for fish that seem to have no interest in food. Always remove food from the tank that has not been consumed.

Try flake food and frozen brine shrimp as your staples and mix in a variety of foods as your fish acclimate to your aquarium. Try not to feed your fish right after turning on the light; they won't be fully alert until about 30 minutes later. In addition, make sure that you match the size of the food with the size of the fish's mouths. You may need to crush or mulch the food for fish with small mouths. Be sure not to grind the food too small. This will add fine particles to the water that will not be digested but will degrade water quality.

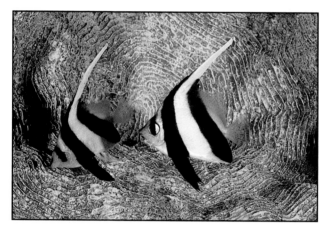

Watch your fish as they eat, inappetence is one of the first symptoms of illness.

If you are going to be away from your aquarium for up to one or two days, the fish will be fine without food. For longer periods, make arrangements for someone to feed your fish. Prepare portions ahead of time and give detailed instructions on how to offer them properly. Do not let them feed your fish at their own discretion unless they are experienced aquarists. Remember that it is better to underfeed than to overfeed your fish.

chapter 7

Maintaining
Your Aquarium

You have planned your aquarium, purchased your equipment, set up your tank, established excellent water quality, carefully selected and introduced the fish and fed them well. Now it is time to maintain the health of your fish by maintaining the quality of their new home. Aquarium maintenance involves everything from turning the light on and off every day and feeding the fish to spending time observing the fish. This latter task is often the most enjoyable. Get to know your fish, watch how they interact and make note of any unusual behavior. Check the fish closely for any signs of disease and watch their interactions to see if any are being picked on.

The more constant you make the conditions in your aquarium, the less likely you are to cause stress to your fish. Rapid fluctuations in water temperature and water quality will cause stress and therefore compromise the health of your fish. You must monitor the water temperature making sure that it remains constant. Check the water level and specific gravity as well. Remember that water should be topped off as often as necessary with tap water. Examine the filter, heater and the airstones to make sure that they are in working order. The thermostat light in the heater should be working prop-

erly. Make sure the air pump and airstones are operating at maximum efficiency. Empty the protein skimmer cup if organic waste has accumulated. These things should be checked daily and require just a few moments of your time. While you are feeding or simply enjoying your pets, you can perform a routine check of the tank components and the aquarium occupants.

One of the most enjoyable tasks associated with aquarium maintenance is observing the fish. (Redhead Goby)

General Maintenance

Cleaning an aquarium involves an active, conscientious effort on your part. In fact, maintaining a fish tank is not for the lazy at heart. Don't set up a tank if you don't intend to follow through and keep it clean and healthy. All too often, interest wanes after the first couple of months, and the aquarium occupants ultimately suffer the consequences. Realize that going into this hobby requires a real commitment on your part. Concern must be shown at every step and on every level. Your fish's lives depend on your attention to detail.

VACUUMING

Vacuuming is one of the most important parts of maintaining your tank. You must reduce the accumulation of mulm or detritus in the gravel so that the under-gravel filter remains effective. Mulm is the combination of fish wastes and uneaten food that decay on the bottom of the aquarium. If not removed, this organic waste will ultimately break down into ammonia and nitrites and overwhelm the nitrogen cycle. This will disturb your water chemistry, potentially harming your fish. If detritus is allowed to accumulate to excessive levels, your filter will be clogged, and water quality will go downhill fast. Too much mulm will clog the under-gravel filter and prevent water flow through the gravel, reducing the filter's efficiency.

A healthy aquar-ium requires diligent mainte-nance, but you will be rewarded with healthy and beautiful fish, like this Scarletfin Wrasse.

Aquarium vacuums, sometimes called substrate cleaners, are commercially available. I recommend using a wide hose to siphon wastes while you are doing a water change. This, in effect, accomplishes two goals at once: vacuuming mulm and removing water from the tank. When you do vacuum make sure that you gently rake the gravel. Don't mix it up too aggressively because this may disrupt the filter.

CHECK THE FILTER

Assuming you have an external filter it is very important to check the filter media. The top level matt gets dirty quickly and easily, as this is the level that collects the largest pieces of debris. An excessive build-up of detritus in your filter will inhibit flow and ultimately reduce the filter's effectiveness.

Rinse the filter matt under lukewarm water every three or four months until the water is clear. You should probably replace about 50 percent of the media every 6 months, making sure to reuse about half of the old filter material. You have established a working bacterial colony in your filter medium and you don't want to throw it out and start from square one. That's why some of the old media must be retained. One of the most common mistakes is the replacement of the entire filter contents every couple of months because it looks dirty. Some of that "dirt" is bacteria beneficial to the filtering process. For filters that utilize cartridges as media, check with the manufacturer for optimum maintenance and replacement rate. The activated carbon in the filter should be good for about two months, then it should be replaced.

ALGAE

Throughout this book, I refer to algae as a friend of the marine aquarium if it does not get out of control. Algae removes nitrate from the water and provides food for some of the naturally herbivorous fishes. What exactly are algae and are all algae beneficial?

Algae are actually plants that belong to the class known as Thallophyta, the same class as fungi. They are relatively simple plants that range in size from the one-celled microscopic types to large seaweeds that grow to over 230 feet. Algae are very hardy and have a tremendous reproductive capacity. They can enter your aquarium as algal spores borne by the air or carried by tank furnishings from another aquarium.

Algae have adapted to all kinds of water conditions. In your aquarium, they can be found on the surface, suspended in the water or on the surfaces of rocks, gravel and tank decorations. There are three groups of algae that are most common to the tropical aquarist:

Green Algae   Only about 10 percent of the green algae are marine forms. These are the most beneficial of the algae. They are green in color because their pigments are identical to those of more evolved plants.

103

This group contains one-celled and multi-celled species. The one-celled green algae are not visible to the naked eye but appear as a green cloudiness in the water. These will sometimes form a green film on the aquarium glass. Multi-celled species also cause the water of your tank to look green. Green algae species form a filamentous mass in the aquarium while others form green threads attached to rocks and plants.

Diatoms These are usually the first algae to establish themselves. They proliferate in aquariums with high nitrate levels, forming a brown slime on the gravel, rocks, decorations and aquarium glass. Heavy concentrations of diatoms will discolor the water. As the aquarium matures, these algae should disappear.

Algae is beneficial in the marine aquarium if it doesn't get out of control.

Blue-green Algae These organisms are actually in a class of their own (Cyanophyceae) because they possess characteristics of both algae and bacteria. In your aquarium, blue-green algae form a dark brown/red gelatinous mat on rocks, gravel and plants. If allowed to proliferate, they will smother the tank. These nuisance algae must be controlled. High nitrate levels and bright light encourage these algae, which can survive in both acidic and alkaline water. They are also capable of producing toxins that will poison aquarium fish. Water that is not well maintained or frequently changed is hospitable to this algae.

At certain levels, algae is beneficial to the aquarium, but it can grow excessively if the conditions are right. Excessive algal growth will overrun a tank unless it is removed. High nitrate levels and sunlight will promote algal growth. Avoiding these conditions will minimize algae as a tank nuisance. If beneficial green algae is excessive, simply remove it from the aquarium fix-tures by rinsing them. A vacuum will help remove it from the gravel. If the excessive algae is the blue-green slime algae, every effort must be made to remove all the algae and its causes. Poor water quality must be improved. Test the water, do a partial water change and check the operation of your filters.

Test the Water

When you first set up the aquarium, testing the water every couple of days is critical to monitoring the maturation process. When you begin to add fish, water chemistry may change radically, and water quality monitoring is critical to the survival of your fish. After this sensitive period of two to four months, it is still very important to test your water, and I recommend that you do so every two weeks. This will give you a good understanding of the mechanics of the nitrogen cycle and will let you know when a water change is needed. Sudden behavioral changes in your fish, fish disease, fish mortality, excessive algal growth and "smelly" or cloudy water all warrant an immediate water quality test and possible water change.

Water Changes

Water changes are one of the most important aspects of cleaning and maintaining your tank. A water change is when you literally take out a percentage of the aquarium water and replace it with properly balanced artificial seawater. The amount you change varies with the quality of your tank and with the frequency of water changes. Some experts feel that 10 percent water change is sufficient every two weeks, while others feel that this volume should be 20 percent. I recommend that you start with a water change of 20 percent every two weeks and adjust this amount depending on water quality.

Water changes help to maintain good water quality because you are diluting the amount of nitrogenous compounds like nitrites and nitrates, harmful gases and other toxic substances each time you do one. The water you add, which should be the proper specific gravity, will replace exhausted trace elements and nutrients as well.

The best way to do a water change is to use a siphon and a large bucket. The siphon is basically just a three- or four-foot hose or tube that will transfer water from the tank to the bucket.

Siphoning.

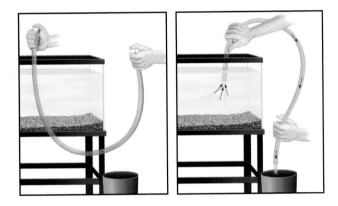

How to Siphon

1. Fill the tube completely with water, making sure there is no trapped air in the tube. Make sure that the siphon is clean and that your hands are clean as well. You can fill the hose by submerging it in the aquarium, but only do this if your aquarium is large enough to accommodate the hose without spooking the fish. Otherwise, place one end of the tube in the tank and apply suction to the other to start the flow.

2. Make sure that the bucket end is lower than the aquarium or siphoning will not work. If you filled your siphon in the aquarium, plug one end of the hose tightly with your thumb, lift it from the aquarium, and bring it lower than the tank to the bucket.

3. Release your thumb and the water will begin to flow rapidly from the aquarium into the bucket.

As I mentioned earlier, use the siphon to remove debris from the tank while you are making a water change. The surface gravel should be stirred just before every partial water change for two reasons. First, it breaks up impacted areas in the filter bed where water flow has become restricted. Second, it puts detritus into suspension where it can be siphoned out with the old water. When it is time to add water try to use aged water that you mixed up and kept stored in a cool dark place. It is also a good idea to aerate the water for a few hours before doing the water change. Make sure that the water you add is the same temperature and specific gravity as that of your aquarium.

MAINTENANCE CHECKLIST

Daily

- Feed the fish twice a day, remove any uneaten food.

- Turn the tank lights on and off.

- Check the water temperature.

- Check the heater and make sure the thermostat light is working.

- Make sure the filter(s) is working properly.

- Make sure the aerator is working properly.

Every other Day

- Check protein skimmer and empty cup if necessary.

- Top up water level with tap water.

- Remove excess algae from glass.

Weekly

- Study the fish closely watching for behavioral changes and signs of disease.

- Check the filter to see if the top matt needs to be replaced.

- Clean cover glasses.

- Measure specific gravity with hydrometer.

Every two weeks
- Change 20 percent of the tank water.

- Vacuum the tank thoroughly and attempt to clean up mulm and detritus.

- Test the water for ammonia, pH, nitrite and nitrate.

Monthly
- Rake through coral sand.

- Rinse any tank decorations that suffer from excess algae.

- Remove excess algae.

Bi-monthly
- Change filter carbon and some floss.

- Clean protein skimmer.

Quarterly (every three months)
- Replace airstones.

- Rinse the filter materials completely and replace some of them if necessary.

In the freshwater aquarium, you are encouraged to do a complete aquarium breakdown every year, essentially starting from scratch. This is not the case in the marine aquarium. The effectiveness of a well-established biological filter will last for years. However, the under-gravel filter may become heavily clogged after a long period of time. The substrate itself may begin to break down as well. If this happens you can slowly replace the gravel over several months by removing a thin strip of gravel and replacing it with new gravel. The next week, repeat the procedure and so on until the entire substrate has been replaced without disrupting the aquarium. Under no circumstances should you break down a healthy aquarium and replace the gravel in one step.

chapter 8

Marine
Tropical Fish
Diseases

If you intend to be a tropical fish hobbyist for some
time, then inevitably one
of your fish will become
infected with some kind of
disease. Marine tropical
fish are subject to all kind
of maladies. Pathogenic
organisms including para-
sites, bacteria, viruses and
fungi are present in all

aquariums. Many are introduced with new fish and many are highly
contagious. However, whether or not diseases actually break out
depends on the resistance of your fish. Poor living conditions will
weaken your fish, cause chronic stress and ultimately lower the fish's
resistance. That's when your fish are most vulnerable to disease.

This is why I have emphasized the importance of maintaining a
healthy aquarium for your pets. Stress caused by capture, handling,
fasting, crowding and injury renders your fish vulnerable to disease.

Nonetheless, you may think you have done everything that you possibly could to have a disease-free environment in your tank, but even the experts experience some problems.

The first step to treating any kind of ailment in your aquarium is to recognize and identify the problem. You will be able to determine that a fish is not healthy by its appearance and behavior. Since you have been spending time examining your fish while you feed them, you will be able to identify problems as soon as they manifest themselves. Telltale behavioral symptoms include: no desire to eat, hyperventilation of the gills, gasping for air near the surface, erratic swimming behavior, lack of movement, rubbing of body or fins and twitching of fins.

External symptoms include a variety of physical abnormalities of the head, body, fins, gills, scales and anus. As I review the various diseases associated with aquarium fish, you will learn what the symptoms of each are.

Commercial Remedies

It is very important that beginners use commercially available treatments instead of homemade remedies. Some experts recommend chemicals like malachite green or potassium permanganate for treating diseases. These chemicals must be handled in very exact dosages. If a fish is overdosed with one of them, it will kill the fish faster than the disease will. Discuss all the possible remedies for a disease with your local pet dealer, and let that person advise you on the best commercial remedies the store carries. If you are still not satisfied, don't be afraid to call your veterinarian and ask a few questions. If your veterinarian does not handle fish, he can usually recommend somebody who does. Finally, when you apply the remedy, make sure that you follow the directions exactly.

Treatment Methods

Unfortunately, the best remedy for disease in the marine aquarium is prevention. Sometimes, despite all your efforts and the application of commercial remedies, the fish will die. Nonetheless, if disease strikes one of your fish, there are a few methods for treating it. These include: direct aquarium treatment with therapeutic agents, the hospital tank, the dip method and internal medication.

DIRECT AQUARIUM TREATMENT

This involves the application of therapeutic agents directly into the tank of the diseased fish. This method is sometimes called the long bath. It can be effective against some diseases, but not always. In some cases, medications may be absorbed by the aquarium decorations or filter media, or they may be toxic to filter bacteria. In these situations, it is best to isolate the infected fish in the hospital tank.

THE HOSPITAL TANK

In an earlier chapter, I mentioned that some aquarists isolate new fish in a quarantine tank. In this way, the fish can be evaluated for signs of disease before introduction into the main aquarium. For your saltwater community tank, I don't recommend a quarantine tank because of the complexities associated with having to maintain two aquariums.

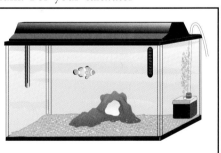

However, I do recommend that you set up a hospital tank to isolate individuals suffering from disease. This tank will reduce the likelihood of the disease spreading to others in the aquarium. It will provide refuge to a fish that may ordinarily be harassed by healthier fish. The hospital tank will make it easier to treat the fish without subjecting other fish to the treatment, and it will make it easier to observe and diagnose the ailing fish.

A hospital tank should be sparse and small, but make sure to include some rocks or flower pots for cover.

The hospital tank need not be large: a 10-gallon tank will do. It does need adequate filtration and aeration, but elaborate decorations and gravel should be left out. For the fish's security, try to provide some kind of cover in the form of rocks or flower pots. An external power filter will be sufficient for the hospital tank.

The Dip Method

This method in itself can be very stressful to the fish. This treatment involves removing the infected fish from the aquarium and dipping it into a bath containing a therapeutic agent or just freshwater. The dip is brief enough not to injure the fish but long enough to kill the pathogen. Unfortunately, this method does not treat the infected agents in the aquarium, just the fish.

The bath is prepared by filling a 1.5-gallon container full of freshwater, matching the temperature and pH of the main aquarium. The pH can be elevated by adding sodium bicarbonate to the container. A quart of seawater should be added to the bath to reduce the osmotic shock to the fish. The fish is netted and placed in the container. It may show signs of disorientation for a moment, but it should recover. Immediately transfer the fish back into the aquarium if it cannot maintain its balance.

Internal Medication

Some remedies need to be administered internally. This is usually accomplished with injection or by feeding the remedy to the fish. The former method is not recommended for the average home aquarist. Feeding the fish food that has been medicated can be very difficult as well. In many cases, the dosage is difficult to estimate, the fish is not feeding normally and you cannot guarantee that the fish being treated is getting the proper amount of food. This treatment method is, therefore, only marginally successful and should be avoided by the beginner.

Common Treatments

The number of treatments available to the home aquarist is somewhat limited for marine fish diseases. The fact of the matter is that many are successful only some of the time. These are generally limited to the administration of copper or antibiotics.

COPPER

Copper is a pollutant in the marine environment. It is, however, thought by many to produce beneficial effects by killing parasites. Copper can have adverse effects on fish, it is not very stable in saltwater systems, and its fate in the aquarium is not fully understood. There are experts who feel that copper should be eliminated as a treatment of aquarium fish diseases. Nonetheless, it is still widely used in the aquarium trade. I would avoid the use of copper for all the reasons stated above unless there are absolutely no alternatives. In this case, I would isolate the fish in a hospital aquarium for treatment.

Only limited treatments are available for marine fish diseases, so the fishkeeper must be extremely careful to keep the aquarium in top condition.

ANTIBIOTICS

Antibiotics are chemotherapeutic agents that seem to be the most effective way of treating some of the common aquarium diseases. When possible, fish should be treated in a hospital tank to avoid the effects of these compounds on a mature established aquarium. Regardless, don't expect miracle cures from these compounds because many have not been found to be fully effective against disease.

Common Aquarium Diseases

There are literally hundreds of possible maladies that can afflict fish. Some are specific to certain species and some can easily be transferred between species. Not all are common in the average home aquarium. The causes of common aquarium ailments may be bacteria, viruses, fungi or parasites.

BACTERIAL DISEASES

Fin Rot

Causes: Aeromonas, *Pseudomonas Vibrio* bacteria.

Symptoms: This is an external bacterial infection that causes erosion or rotting of the fins and the fin rays. The base of the fins usually reddens as well. In advanced stages, the disease spreads to the gills causing bleeding and ulceration to the skin.

Treatment: The occurrence of this disease is thought to reflect deteriorating water quality. Immediate steps should be taken to improve water quality. Remove uneaten food, do a partial water change, change the activated carbon in your filter. The antibiotics furanace, augmentin and ciprofloxin may be effective.

Fish Tuberculosis, Wasting Disease

Causes: *Mycobacterium* bacteria.

Symptoms: External signs of this disease are often lacking. A fish that seems outwardly healthy may be internally infected. Fish that are infected may live a year or

more before succumbing. Skin lesions, emaciation, labored breathing, scale loss, frayed fins and loss of appetite are all clinical signs of this disease. Unfortunately, by the time these are manifested, it is probably too late to save the fish.

Treatment: These bacteria are transmitted orally through raw

Some beneficial bacteria help to fuel the nitrogen cycle in your aquarium, but harmful bacteria can cause severe illness in your fish (French Angelfish).

infected fish flesh, detritus and the feces of infected fish. These bacteria can also infect skin wounds and lesions. The best treatment is prevention; avoid feeding raw fish and shellfish to your aquarium occupants. Antibiotics including kanamycin, erythromycin and streptomycin have shown some promise against these bacteria if the disease is diagnosed. If the aquarium is heavily infected with this disease, it must be sterilized and the water discarded.

Vibriosis, Ulcer Disease

Cause: *Vibrio* bacteria

Symptoms: There is a variety of symptoms associated with this disease depending on the species of *Vibrio* and the species of fish. Symptoms include: lethargy; darkening of color; anemia; ulcers on the skin and lower jaw; bleeding of the gills, skin and intestinal tract; clouded eyes; loose scales; pale gills and sudden death.

Treatment: These bacteria commonly inhabit the intestinal tracts of healthy fish. They only become dangerous when stress allows infection. Poor water quality, crowding, excessive handling and copper treatments are common causes of stress in aquarium fish. Immersion treatments with antibiotic compounds including furanace, erythromycin, halquinol and nitrofurazone have met with some success.

VIRAL DISEASES

Cauliflower Disease, Lymphocystis

Causes: *Cystivirus* virus

Symptoms: Fin and body lesions that are raised, whitish, warty and have a lumpy texture like cauliflower. These lesions may take 3 to 4 weeks to reach their full size. Diseased fish typically show few signs of distress and continue to feed and behave normally. The infection is generally not fatal, but it can be transmitted to other fish in the tank.

Treatment: There is no effective treatment of this viral infection other than to isolate the fish immediately and let the fish's immune system deal with it. This can take up to several months.

FUNGAL DISEASES

Ichthyophonus Disease, Whirling Disease

Causes: *Ichthyphonus* fungus.

Symptoms: These fungi invade the internal organs of the fish, infecting the kidney, heart, spleen and liver. Clinical signs include emaciation, spinal curvature, darkening or paling of the skin, roughening of the skin, fin erosion and skin ulcers. Erratic swimming behavior can be a symptom as well. Necropsy after death reveals white nodules on the internal organs.

Treatment: This fungus is a parasitic organism with a complex life cycle. The fungal cysts are usually ingested by the fish after which they burst, entering the bloodstream and infecting internal organs. Typically, fish with this disease will die up to two months after infestation. Treatment is very difficult due to the internal nature of this disease. The infected fish should be immediately removed from the aquarium to prevent other fish from becoming infected.

Exophiala Disease
Cause: *Exophiala* fungus.

Symptoms: Lethargy, disorientation, and abnormal swimming are signs of this fungal infection.

Treatment: This is a poorly known fungus and no treatment is known. You should isolate the fish to prevent other fish in the aquarium from contracting the fungus.

PARASITIC DISEASES
Marine Velvet Disease
Causes: The dinoflagellate protozoan *Amyloodinium ocellatum.*

Symptoms: The gills are usually the first site of the infection that then spreads to the skin, making it dull, patchy and velvetlike; white spots are visible on sections of intact skin. As the disease progresses, the fish's behavior may include fasting, gasping, scratching against objects and sluggishness. Lesions caused by the dinoflagellate can lead to secondary bacterial infection.

Treatment: This organism has three stages to its life cycle; one of them is parasitic. No completely effective treatment is known, although some antibiotics are effective. These include: malachite green, nitrofurazone and acriflavin. The freshwater dip sometimes dislodges these parasites from the host, but does not kill them. Treatments are often prolonged, and the entire tank must be treated to fully eradicate the infestation.

Marine White Spot, Cryptocaryoniasis, Marine Ich

Causes: The ciliate protozoan *Cryptocaryon irritans*.

Symptoms: Early signs include fasting, cloudy eyes, troubled breathing, excess skin mucus and pale skin. Then white spots appear on the skin, gills and eyes; death follows within a few days most likely due to gill damage.

Treatment: The white spot organism can be very difficult to control. Like marine velvet, the encysted stage of this parasite is resistant to most treatments and remains in the gravel of the aquarium. The freshwater dip may be effective in killing the parasites on the fish but does little to treat the aquarium. Therefore, it is necessary to maintain levels of treatment in the tank. Copper products seem to have limited effectiveness and the antibiotic chloramin T has been used as well.

Uronema

Causes: The ciliate protozoan *Uronema marinum*.

Symptoms: External ulcers, muscle and skin bleeding, lethargic behavior, sloughing of the skin and internal infection are signs of this disease. Death may be rapid due to impaired circulation in the gills.

Treatment: Little is known of this parasite, and there is no known treatment.

Tang Turbellarian Disease, Black Spot

Causes: *Paravortex* flatworms.

Symptoms: Although the name implies that only tangs are infected, this is not the case. Many species of fish can be infected by this flatworm. In the parasitic phase these organisms look like numerous dark spots distributed unevenly over the fins, gills and body. Other signs include fasting, listlessness, pale or whitish skin and scratching against objects. Secondary bacterial infections can occur as well. These signs are common to other infestations by flatworms.

Treatment: Flatworms are in a class of their own, Platyhelminthes. As with most parasitic infestations, crowding facilitates spreading to other tankmates. The freshwater dip, trochlorfon and praziquantel immersion may be effective.

Trematode Infestations

Causes: Monogenetic trematode worms.

Symptoms: Many species of these worms are too small to see without a microscope. They normally infect the gills, eyes, skin, mouth and anal opening. Infected fish usually rub themselves against objects in the aquarium trying to dislodge these parasites, which often causes damage that leads to secondary bacterial infections.

Treatment: These infestations are difficult to eradicate because the life cycles of these animals are poorly understood. Immersion in freshwater, mebendazole, praziquantel, or trichlorfon have been effective against trematodes.

Crustacean Infestations

Causes: Copepod, Isopod and Argulid crustaceans.

Symptoms: Most of these tiny crablike organisms are visible to the naked eye. Copepods will remain fixed in the same position while argulids will move over the surface of the host. Both groups feed by piercing the host, causing tissue damage. Fish with heavy infestations swim erratically, rub against objects and jump. Bacteria will infect resulting lesions.

Treatment: Remove fish that are infested with these parasites immediately. Also remove aquarium decorations and either dry them to kill egg masses or immerse them in 2 percent Clorox solution for 2 hours. Treat infested fish by immersing them in trichlorfon or malathion baths.

Head and Lateral Line Erosion

Cause: Poor water quality, nutrient deficiency or a possible parasite.

Symptoms: As in the freshwater disease hole-in-the-head, holes develop and enlarge in the sensory pits of the head and down the lateral line on the body. The disease progresses slowly and the fish does not seem to behave differently. Advanced stages can lead to secondary bacterial infection and death.

Treatment: There are no specific treatments for this disease although some experts recommend the use of the freshwater antibiotic flagyl. Check your water quality and make necessary adjustments. You should also make sure that you are meeting the nutritional needs of your fish. Diversify their diet and add vitamin supplements to their food.

Fish infected with parasites will rub themselves against objects in the aquarium in an attempt to dislodge the pests.(Midas Blenny).

Poisoning

Causes: Multiple causes including build-up of nitrogenous compounds (ammonia, nitrite), household chemicals (smoke, cleaners, fumes) and tap water constituents (heavy metals, chloramine).

Symptoms: Low levels of toxins in the aquarium will stress fish, thereby lowering their resistance to other diseases. Higher levels will cause abnormal behavior including darting movements, jumping and gasping at the surface.

Treatment: Make sure that activated carbon is being used to remove toxins and conduct a 20–40 percent water change. If pollutant levels are high, move the fish to the hospital tank until the main aquarium water problems are corrected.

part four

Beyond
the
Basics

Specialty
Tanks

Hopefully, this book is just
the beginning for you. It
has provided the founda-
tion that will help you move
on to more sophisticated
aquarium setups. The com-
munity tank is a compila-
tion of fish from diverse
areas cohabitating peace-
fully. Although the community aquarium can be an
intriguing addition to your

home, serious aquarists generally strive for more natural aquarium
setups. They will often set up what is referred to as a specialty tank.
The specialty tank can be a species tank in that it may house only one
kind of fish, but generally it contains multiple species of fish originating from one area. In essence, the specialty tank makes every
effort to fully mimic one particular habitat. It contains fish from
that habitat, invertebrates from that habitat and substrate and decorations that mimic that habitat.

Specialty tanks are beyond the scope of this book. However, for the
serious aquarist who has mastered the basics with a community

aquarium and would like to venture into the world of specialty tanks, I recommend some of the books listed in chapter 11. In these books, the authors review the many types of fish habitats that can be re-created in your home. Among them are: the general community tank described in this book, the cool temperate water aquarium and the tropical Hawaiian coral reef. These aquariums may be fish-only, invertebrate-only or mixed fish and invertebrate. These are just a sampling of the types of specialty tanks that can be created. Each habitat has its own group of resident species that live in harmony within that habitat. In addition, putting together a marine specialty tank does not require making large changes in your water chemistry, though you must be sure that your water is pristine if you are going to add invertebrates. Unlike freshwater habitats, the characteristics of seawater are not radically different among the coral reefs around the world. Therefore, if you intend to stick with a tropical aquarium, you need only consider changing the species composition and some of the decorations to construct a specialty tank. When the specialty tank is finished, you will have re-created another part of the world within your home.

A coral reef aquarium might include fantastic creatures like this Greek Goddess sea slug.

The specialty tank is not your only avenue of expansion in this hobby. You may want to try to maintain some of the more difficult species of fish listed in chapter 5. You can also start to introduce invertebrates into your tank. You can expand your fish's diets by culturing your own foods like I outlined in chapter 6. There is so much you can do as an aquarist.

chapter 10

Resources
for the **Aquarist**

Home aquarists number in the millions throughout the world. As you become more involved in aquarium keeping, you will be surprised at how many people share this exciting hobby. Growing up, many of my friends had aquariums, and we would spend hours working with the tank and its occupants. Later, I found myself going to my local pet dealer just to see new fish arrivals, to talk about aquarium problems and to exchange ideas with fellow aquarists. I have picked up some of the most valuable information on fishkeeping from amateurs who enjoy the thrills of this hobby.

Clubs

In many areas, aquarium enthusiasts have formed clubs and associations where ideas and techniques are endlessly bantered about. You can find out about these organizations by asking your local pet dealer. Not only are these kinds of organizations great for gathering information, but you may also be able to buy used equipment as well as healthy homebred fish.

Books

Literally thousands of books have been published on
every facet of aquarium keeping. The bibliography in
the back of this chapter is a mere smattering of what is
available for the new and experienced aquarist. Each
one of those books listed has its own bibliography
which will help you to delve further into the field.
Books have been written to address virtually every
aspect of the hobby. They cover broad topics like basic
aquarium set-up and very specialized topics like the
proper husbandry of a certain species. If you have any
question about aquarium keeping, it is covered in a
book.

Magazines

Monthly aquarium magazines provide you with some
of the most up-to-date information on aquarium
keeping. Timely articles on breeding, feeding, disease
and species specific husbandry will both entertain
and inform the new aquarist. Product information
and classified advertising are excellent features of the
aquarium magazine. Two such magazines which have
proven to be very good conduits of information are:
Aquarium Fish Magazine (P.O. Box 53351, Boulder, CO
80322, 303-666-8504) and *Tropical Fish Hobbyist* (One
TFH Plaza, Neptune City, NJ 07753, 908-988-8400).

Internet

Yes, fishkeeping has even entered the computer age.
This is probably the fastest way to obtain and exchange
information on aquarium keeping. If you have access
to the Internet, then you have unlimited access to a
vast amount of information on fishkeeping. Some
Internet access companies have even established net-
works for fish enthusiasts which you can join. One such
network is Fishnet by Compuserve (800-524-3388).
Membership in this network gives you access to hobbyists, professional aquarists, researchers, breeders and
vendors of aquarium products. You can even get immediate advice from staff about sick fish.

chapter 11

Bibliography

Bailey, M. and G. Sandford. *The Ultimate Aquarium.* New York: Smithmark Publishers, 1995.

Bower, C.E. *The Basic Marine Aquarium.* Springfield: Charles C. Thomas Publishing, 1983.

Burgess, W.E. *Marine Aquariums: A Complete Introduction.* Neptune City: TFH Publications, 1989.

Burgess, W.E., H.R. Axelrod, R.E. Hunziker III. *Atlas of Marine Aquarium Fishes.* Neptune City: TFH Publications, 1990.

Dakin, N. *The Macmillan Book of the Marine Aquarium.* New York: Macmillan Publishing Co., 1992.

Eschmeyer, W. M. *Catalogue of the Genera of Recent Fishes.* San Francisco: California Academy of Sciences, 1990.

Kay, G. *The Tropical Marine Fish Survival Manual.* London: Quarto Inc., 1995.

Lundegaard, G. *Keeping Marine Fish: An Aquarium Guide.* New York: Sterling Publishing Co., 1991.

Melzak, M. *The Marine Aquarium Manual.* New York: Arco Publishing Inc., 1984.

Mills, D. *Aquarium Fish.* New York: Dorling Kindersley Publishing, 1993.

Moyle, P. B. and J. J. Cech, Jr. *Fishes: An Introduction to Ichthyology.* Englewood Cliffs: Prentice-Hall Inc., 1982.

Sandford, G. *An Illustrated Encyclopedia of Aquarium Fish.* New York: Howell Book House, 1995.

Scott, P. W. *The Complete Aquarium.* New York: Dorling Kindersley Publishing, 1995.

Spotte, S. *Captive Seawater Fishes: Science and Technology.* New York: John Wiley and Sons, 1992.

Spotte, S. *Seawater Aquariums.* New York: John Wiley and Sons, 1979.

Stoskopf, M. K. *Fish Medicine.* Philadelphia: W.B. Saunders Co., 1993.